THINK:ACT

'think:act–Leadership Know-how' is derived from the academic research and the consulting experience of Roland Berger Strategy Consultants, one of the world's leading strategy consultancies. With 36 offices in 25 countries, the company has successful operations in all major international markets. Roland Berger Strategy Consultants serve global players and innovative companies as well as public institutions and governments. In 2009, our services generated more than €616 million in revenues with 2,000 employees. The strategy consultancy is an independent partnership exclusively owned by about 180 Partners. This series of management books is based on the success of our international business magazine think: act that covers all aspects of leadership challenges and is published in Chinese, Russian, English, German and Polish.

Dedication

*To my wife Valérie,
my daughters Laure-Victoire and Charlotte-Alicia,
and my other loved ones,
for all they have given me.*

China's Management Revolution

Spirit, land, energy

Charles-Edouard Bouée

First published 2011 by
PALGRAVE MACMILLAN

Palgrave Macmillan in the UK is an imprint of Macmillan Publishers Limited,
registered in England, company number 785998, of Houndmills, Basingstoke,
Hampshire RG21 6XS.

Palgrave Macmillan in the US is a division of St Martin's Press LLC,
175 Fifth Avenue, New York, NY 10010.

Palgrave Macmillan is the global academic imprint of the above companies
and has companies and representatives throughout the world.

Palgrave® and Macmillan® are registered trademarks in the United States,
the United Kingdom, Europe and other countries

ISBN 978-0-230-28545-3

This book is printed on paper suitable for recycling and made from fully
managed and sustained forest sources. Logging, pulping and manufacturing
processes are expected to conform to the environmental regulations of the
country of origin.

A catalogue record for this book is available from the British Library.

A catalog record for this book is available from the Library of Congress.

10 9 8 7 6 5 4 3
20 19 18 17 16 15 14 13 12 11

Printed and bound in Great Britain by
MPG Group, Bodmin and Kings Lynn

Contents

Table

Boxes

ACKNOWLEDGMENTS

This book has been germinating for several years, during which time my views on how businesses are managed in China have been influenced by conversations with many people. I am grateful to all of them, and particularly to the nine entrepreneurs whose profiles are included in the pages that follow—Feng Jun, Jiang Xipei, John Deng, Ye Maozhong, Yuan Yafei, Zhang Lan, Zhang Yong, Zhou Hongyi, and Zong Qinghou—and to Guo Zhenxi, director of CCTV-2. They are all busy people, and I count it as a great privilege that they were interested enough in my thesis to spare the time to talk at length to me and Luyang Jiang about their businesses and their styles of management.

I also want to thank the academics and media friends with whom I have had the chance to discuss my ideas, particularly Professor David Garvin, of Harvard Business School, for sparing me the time to exchange ideas on western and Chinese management in both Shanghai and Boston, Mass.

I also owe a great debt of gratitude to members of my staff (my "light *dong ban*") in Shanghai and Beijing for their enthusiastic help during the project, particularly to Sophia Huang for her diligent and valuable research and perceptive comments on the early drafts, and to Shelley Zhang for her supremely efficient administrative support.

I would also like to take this opportunity to thank Grace Qian, my personnel director, and Qian Fang, my CFO, for helping me, with their wise counsel, to learn how to be a good Chinese leader. A special thanks also to my Chinese partners who demonstrate the Chinese management style everyday in our joint work with Chinese clients. Thanks also to my assistant in Paris, Caroline Gendey, who helps me to keep my balance with one foot in China and the other in France.

Thanks to Christiane Diekmann for managing the European end of what was a complicated, polyglot project in a way that suggested she would have made a great career diplomat, and also for her insights into and advice on the structure of the book, and her invariably apposite comments on the drafts. And thanks to Torsten

Oltmanns, not only for asking me over lunch one day in December 2008 to write a book on China, but also for providing me with the team and resources I needed to do it.

Very special thanks are due to two people, Luyang Jiang and Tom Lloyd. Luyang has supported and helped me to develop the thesis from the outset, and has remained committed to the project throughout. She suggested most of the interview subjects, organized the interview program, did the interviews with me or by herself, wrote them up, and took most of the pictures. Her insights and network, her constructive criticism, her interest in and knowledge about Chinese entrepreneurs, and her fine photographer's eye have all been invaluable.

In addition to helping me with the writing, Tom helped me to develop my ideas in regular brainstorming sessions, did much of the research, and contributed his deep knowledge of management models and history. I thank him for sharing this journey of discovery with me in China, while adhering to his own convictions, for managing the timing and deadlines, and for the enjoyment of working together.

Finally, my thanks to Stephen Rutt at Palgrave Macmillan for agreeing do to the book and to Susan Curran for deft editing.

A few weeks after the outbreak of the Second World War on September 1, 1939, the prime minister Winston Churchill told the British people in a radio broadcast, 'I cannot forecast to you the action of Russia. It is a riddle, wrapped in a mystery, inside an enigma ....' Those attempting to forecast developments in China, including many Chinese, feel the same bafflement and perplexity. That China will be a great economic power there is no doubt, but what kind of power will it be? As the faces of its people are to westerners, China is inscrutable, particularly now, as China's rich and ancient culture ponders, processes, and digests the lessons and implications of the 2008 global crisis.

This book is written by a European who lives in China, and advises some of China's largest companies. It is an attempt to shed light on an unexpected development that the author believes is of vital importance to companies dealing in any way with Chinese businesses or businesspeople: the gradual emergence, from all this pondering and digestion, of a new style of business management.

It does not play the Chinese numbers game; does not extrapolate from China's economic progress over the past 30 years, for instance, to predict its share of world output in 2038. Its focus is not on the growing economic might of China, but on signs that the interaction between its culture, system of government, and the restless energy of its entrepreneurs will change the way the world does business.

It would, of course, be presumptuous in the extreme for a European who has worked in China for less than five years to claim anything approaching intimacy with the culture of one of the world's great civilizations. Chinese people and western Sinologists are bound to find some errors, misunderstandings, and mis-spellings in the pages that follow. They are mine and I apologize for them in advance. It will not, however, be seen as presumptuous, I hope, for a Global Executive Committee member of a leading strategy consulting firm, who is an alumnus of Harvard Business School and is working in China, to express views on how western management concepts, principles, and tools are being perceived and digested in China. Sometimes the outsider can see things more clearly than the insider.

The Chinese management style is not being crafted deliberately. It is emerging from the attempts of some of China's entrepreneurs to find better ways to manage their companies. They are "going with the flow" as the Daoists advocate, but in so doing, I believe, they are creating something new, and of great significance for business everywhere.

Charles-Edouard Bouée
Shanghai, July 2010

China is generally thought in the West to have ridden out the 2008 financial crisis largely unscathed. Exports fell as the economies of China's main trading partners went into recession, and economic growth eased a percentage point or two, as a consequence. But the economy as a whole continued to grow throughout the recession, and unlike those of other developed countries, China's public finances remained healthy.

Economic and financial appearances are deceptive.

China was profoundly shocked by the crisis. As a senior government official said in the autumn of 2008, "China is waking up from a 30-year dream. Everything we believed in has crashed."

The dream that has beguiled China since Deng Xiaoping launched the great opening up in 1978 is the American Dream. The Chinese people wanted China to be the new America; even larger, even richer, even stronger. And they pursued the dream with the zeal of converts for three decades.

It worked. China has become a great, although not yet the greatest, economic power, and has given the lie to sceptics who warned that US-style *laissez-faire* capitalism could not work in the absence of its political counterpart, liberal democracy.

But now that their American idol/model has turned out to have feet of clay (or of sub-prime mortgages) and the supposed stability and adaptability of free markets have proved illusory, China's leading thinkers, policy-makers, and business people have begun to reflect and reassess.

Nothing could be more important for firms operating or planning to operate in China, and businesses whose fates are linked in one way or another and to a greater or lesser extent to China, than to try to understand the debates, discussions, heart-searching, and also the sense of liberation, that the rude awakening from the American Dream has inspired, and what new models of business, management, and economic development might emerge from them.

China has not been left bewildered and rudderless by its erstwhile paragon's fall from grace. Confidence is running high, despite the shock of the global crisis. A triumphant Beijing Olympic Games, at which China won more gold medals than the United States, a successful space programme, a growing sense of economic might, and buoyant domestic capital markets have combined to create a sense that China stands on its own as a strong nation with no allegiance to foreign creeds or cultures.

This new self-confidence and sense of independence are also evident in business, and particularly within a group of private Chinese entrepreneurs who, although they acknowledge the strengths of the western management model, and the usefulness of many of its tools and principles, doubt its general applicability to China. Profiles of some of them are included in the pages that follow. They are not "revolutionaries," in the sense that they're rejecting all of what some of them learned at western business schools. They are adapting (or rather retro-fitting) the western management model and style to modern China and infusing it with ideas, concepts, philosophies, and spiritual themes derived from China's culture. In the process, they are bringing about, mostly unconsciously, what may be seen in retrospect as a revolution in business management.

It is this quiet revolution, still in its very early stages, that is the focus of this book.

The book is divided into three parts. The first part covers what I call "the American experiment." It begins, in Chapter 1, "The road from isolation," with a brief account of how the policy of economic liberalism adopted by Deng Xiaoping in 1978, combined with China's communist, one-party system of government to produce four kinds of Chinese enterprise.

Chapter 2, "2008, the turning point," describes the reactions of the Chinese people to the Sichuan earthquake in May 2008, and suggests that it revealed to the outside world a new China, very different from the China of 1978. I argue that this new China, combined with the growing self-confidence of the Chinese people, and the growing disenchantment with the American model, deepened by the 2008 world financial crisis, has brought the American experiment to an end.

Part II, "Spirit, land, energy," describes the origins of a new style of management that I see emerging in China, after the end of the American experiment. It begins in Chapter 3 with an account of how management styles evolve that casts doubt on the common assumption that the western style of management is the "best" style. Chapters 4, "Spirit," 5, "Land," and 6, "Energy," each deal with one key attribute of the environment within which this new, Chinese management style is emerging.

Part III, "Crossing the river," examines China's management revolution and its implications for companies. Chapter 7, "Chinese management," explores nine distinctive features of this emerging Chinese style of management, and explains why it emphasizes "vision and tactics" and assigns a subordinate role to "strategy." Chapter 8, "Strangers in a strange land," explores the implications of the Chinese style of management for foreign companies. Chapter 9, "Two roads ahead," ends the book, by summarizing the argument, and urging Chinese and western business people to try harder to understand each other.

In an interview in *Le Figaro* on June 8, 2010 ("Haier sacré empereur chinois du réfrigérateur") Zhang Ruimin, CEO of Haier, the world's fourth largest white goods manufacturer based in Qingdao, Shandong Province, acknowledged the problem. "Le plus difficile pour nous," he said, "est de faire comprendre notre philosophie de management à nos dirigeants locaux" (the most difficult thing for us is to get our local managers to understand our management philosophy).

I hope this book goes some way towards improving the understanding of western business people of China, and vice versa. Its purpose is not to describe the emerging Chinese style of management in any detail (since it is emerging, that would be futile), but to explain why it is emerging, to give an impression of its flavor and shape, and to suggest that, although it is a creature of the environment for business in China in the early twenty-first century, it might incorporate features that western managers could learn from.

Part I

The American experiment (1978–2008)

CHAPTER 1

The road from isolation

In August 2003, in Chengdu, in south-west China's Sichuan province, a telephone number consisting of eight eights was sold at auction for 2.33 million yuan (about US$280,723). The opening ceremony of China's Olympics Games in Beijing on the eighth day of the eighth month (August 8) of 2008, began at 8 seconds and 8 minutes past 8 pm local time.

Eight is a lucky number in China. The word for "eight" sounds like the word for "prosper," or "wealth." In regional dialects, such as Cantonese, "eight" sounds like the word for "fortune."

One of the most significant and, in the view of most Chinese, most auspicious years in the history of modern China was 1978. Bruised and battered by the two disasters of the Great Leap Forward (1958–62), during which 30–40 million people died in famines following the collectivization of farming, and the great leap backward known as the Cultural Revolution (1966–76), during which hundreds of thousands of China's intellectuals were killed or driven into exile, China was searching for a new direction.

It was provided by Deng Xiaoping, one of the greatest statesmen of the twentieth century. He and other pragmatists in the Chinese Communist Party (CCP) had had some success in restoring the economy to some kind of health following the Great Leap Forward. But Deng and Liu Shaoqi, who had replaced Mao Zedong as chairman of the CCP in 1962, lost power on the return of a rejuvenated Mao at the head of the Great Proletarian Cultural Revolution.

Deng was accused of unleashing a "capitalist windstorm" by calling for peasants to be given back their plots of land, because, as he famously put it, "it doesn't matter if a cat is black or white; if it can catch mice [farm land efficiently] it is a good cat."

Box 1.1 Deng Xiaoping (1904–1997)

Deng was brought up on a farm in Guang'an, in Sichuan province. He studied in France during the 1920s, and joined the CCP in 1923. On returning to China, he became a political commissar in rural areas and was a "revolutionary veteran" of the Long March. After the PRC came to power in 1949 Deng worked in Tibet and other south-western regions to consolidate Communist control. He was deeply involved in the economic reconstruction following the Great Leap Forward in the early 1960s.

Deng was known for being "three times up and down," because he was "purged" three times; once before 1949, once during the Cultural Revolution, and again in 1976. He was regarded as a "tough little man" in the West, and was seen by Chinese people as someone who had strong beliefs and never gave up.

He was head of the "second generation" of the CCP's leadership and the architect of "Socialism, with Chinese characteristics." He was instrumental in opening Shanghai's Pudong New Area, which made the city China's economic hub. Some of his sayings seem so prosaic now that it is easy to forget how shocking and inspirational they must have been to a people used to the ideological rigours of the Great Proletarian Cultural Revolution. He said that the "leftist" elements of Chinese society were much more dangerous than "rightist" ones, and his declaration that "to get rich is glorious" unleashed a wave of entrepreneurship that continues to drive China's economy today.

One of Deng's most important legacies in the view of many Chinese people, and one of his own most cherished wishes, was the return of Hong Kong to China. It is considered a great sadness that Deng died four months before that dream was finally realized.

After Mao died in 1976, Deng and like-minded CCP members embarked on reform.

The American model

Deng was the consummate pragmatist, and his famous black and white cat aphorism, a quintessential pragmatist's credo, became a slogan for the "Four Modernizations"—of agriculture, industry, science and technology, and national defence—that he and his fellow reformers embarked on in 1978. But Deng's allegiance was to communism and to the CCP, of which he became the paramount leader, not to pragmatism itself. It was already clear by 1978 that the Soviet Union, the inspiration of the CCP since its formation in the early 1920s, was a failing economic experiment threatened by severe pressures, both external and internal. Deng realized that if the party was not to become vulnerable to similar threats of implosion and explosion, another economic system, a cat of a different color that put more trust in the natural entrepreneurialism of the Chinese people, was needed.

In a speech delivered on June 30, 1984, Deng admitted that "one of our shortcomings after the founding of the People's Republic, was that we did not pay enough attention to developing the productive forces. Socialism means eliminating poverty." But how should these "productive forces" be encouraged?

Deng had visited Japan in 1972, and been impressed by the speed of Japan's post-war economic recovery. He returned in 1978 as China's leader, and met Japanese entrepreneurs and economists, as well as the emperor. In the early years of his leadership Japan's economic miracle was a potent symbol for Deng of what was possible, but the model of economic development he chose for China, which was also Japan's post-war model, was the American model. After the collapse of the Soviet Union and the advent of the unipolar world, China's relationships with the United States were strengthened further.

It must have seemed to China's leaders that the American model had much to commend it in 1978. The United States was in the process of vanquishing its only rival, Soviet communism. It was an easier, purer brand of capitalism to copy than the more complicated European version, and the American Dream—work hard, make money, be who you want to be—may have seemed, to China's leadership, to be the kind of dream that would unleash the entrepreneurial energy China needed to fuel its growth. "Poverty isn't socialism," Deng said later. "To be rich is glorious." His idea was to allow some of the people to get rich first, to encourage others to follow their example.

Whatever their reasons, China's leaders took a bet on the US model in 1978, and have persisted with it subsequently through thick and thin, through good times and bad. They and their successors have adapted it here and there, to the cultural and industrial legacies they inherited, and made it work for China.

The modernizations

The new government's first step in 1978 was to return to business left unfinished at the onset of the Cultural Revolution, and allow the break-up of the collective farms created during the Great Leap Forward.

In November 1978, 18 farmers of Xiaogang village, Fengyang county in Anhui province, signed a secret agreement with thumb-prints to divide the land of the local commune into household plots. Because such a division was strictly forbidden at that time, the contract stipulated that if any signatories were beheaded or imprisoned for this violation of Mao's collectivization laws, the other villagers would take care of their children until they were 18.

Xiaogang villagers were close to starvation in 1978. Residents had to get by on a meager 50 kg per head of grain a year, not because Xiaogang land was infertile, but because the commune's production team decided all matters relating to land, and farmers had little incentive to work hard. "All we wanted was to feed our families," a signatory recalled later. "If we could provide enough food, it was OK even if we ended up beheaded."

In 1979 the village's grain output was 90,000 kg, roughly equal to all the harvests of the previous 20 years, and Xiaogang delivered seven times its fixed quota to the government. Income per villager was 400 yuan, 18 times the previous year and almost four times the national average income for farmers.

The model was copied by neighbouring villages, and soon word of the illegal experiment reached Beijing. Instead of losing their heads or their freedom, the 18 farmers became heroes, the experiment was officially approved, and Xiaogang was dubbed "Number One village of China's reform." Four years later Deng introduced the "Household Contract Responsibility System," which sanctioned family plots and allowed farmers to grow whatever crops they wanted, and sell their surpluses.

By then, grain production had risen by a third since 1978, and the variety of produce had increased substantially. Surpluses replaced previously persistent shortages, and many entrepreneurial farmers used them to start sideline businesses. In seven years the average income of rural households trebled. One consequence of this rapid increase in agricultural efficiency was that millions of Chinese people previously tied to the land became mobile and available for employment in companies and the industrial sector.

The Xiaogang story, and the fact that it is the officially approved account of the origins of the agricultural reforms, illustrates an important feature of Deng's approach to the "four modernizations." Although a fervent communist and centralist politically, Deng was a fervent liberal, almost an anarchist, economically. He saw in the farmers of Xiaogang not law-breakers, but personifications of China's entrepreneurial spirit, and he was willing to follow where that spirit led.

Unleashing productive forces

The policy designed to effect the other three "modernizations" was Deng's great opening up to the outside world. Low-tax, zero import duty Special Economic Zones (SEZs) were established, to attract foreign investors. Three of these new SEZs, in Shenzhen, Zhuhai, and Shantou, were in Guangdong (Canton) and bordered the economically vibrant British crown colony of Hong Kong (which was returned to China in 1997). In 1980, the average factory wage in Hong Kong was about eight times the average factory wage in Guangdong. This difference was not lost on the Hong Kong business community. They opened many thousands of factories in Guangdong, and employed several millions of mainland Chinese. By the mid-1980s Guangdong had taken off, and overtaken Shanghai as China's largest exporting region. Small towns burgeoned into thriving industrial centres. Shenzhen was transformed within a few years from a small fishing port, with a population of 70,000, into a major industrial city.[1]

Other regions wanted in. In 1982, 14 more coastal towns were given SEZ status, and a year later several more were made "open economic regions," including the Pearl River delta.

But not all of China's entrepreneurs were flocking to the SEZs.

In a fascinating and unexpected sequel to the Xiaogang story, farmers began to use the surpluses they accumulated following the break-up of the collective farms in 1978 to start small businesses on the *qian dian, hou chang* (shop in front, factory behind) model. This term was used to describe relationships between mainland factories on the Pearl River delta (*hou chang*) and Hong Kong (*qian dan*).

Most remained small, because the law prevented them from employing more than five workers and borrowing money for expansion, but some contrived to liberate themselves from such constraints by adapting a local enterprise model introduced during the Great Leap Forward.

Township and Village Enterprises (TVEs), as they came to be known, were originally commune-run ventures created to supply rural areas with staples such as iron, steel, cement, fertilizer, farm tools, and hydroelectric power. Following the 1978 reforms they attracted the interest of qian dian, hou chang entrepreneurs, because they could employ as many people as they liked provided they complied with the commune requirement to give a quarter of their profits to employees.

TVEs were "collectively owned," but "use rights" were delegated to managers in an arrangement that led some observers to describe TVE property rights as "fuzzy." So they were, but the story of China's walk across the river between communist politics and capitalist economics makes fuzziness appear more of a virtue than a vice. In this case, fuzzy property rights allowed the TVEs to accommodate a variety of "stakeholders," adapt to a wide range of situations, and develop, in some cases, into large and successful enterprises.

A few TVEs were run by local governments, but many were in reality private enterprises masquerading as publicly owned collectives for political, legal, and regulatory reasons. During the early years of reform, when the idea of "private" enterprise was hard to digest in communist China, there was much to be said for using collectively owned vehicles for essentially capitalist enterprise.

This masquerade came to be known as *dai hing maozi* (donning the red hat). "Red hat" companies were not confined to TVEs. Another version was the "hang-on household enterprise," with equally fuzzy status – a private business that pretended to be the offshoot of a state-owned enterprise (SOE) so that it could borrow money from state-owned banks and escape tax.

But there was a price to pay for this fuzzy fudging of the awkward task of thrusting the square peg of capitalist enterprise into the round hole of socialism. The equivocal legal status and property rights of red hat companies meant that they required lubricants to make them work, in the form of bribes, back-handers, turning blind eyes, and close relationships between merchants and administrators. Some see this as a modern version of China's time-honored system of networking (*guanxi*), advocated by Confucius as a social stabilizer. Others see it as corruption, plain and simple. The Chinese government has been among the latter, and has made the fight against corruption a high priority.

This is not to excuse or belittle China's persistently high ranking in international corruption league tables. Corruption is always bad for business, because it discourages entrepreneurs and leads to an inefficient allocation of resources. It is simply to explain that socialism and capitalism are awkward bedfellows, and putting them together in China imposed exceptional strains on standards of business ethics, particularly in the TVE sector.

TVEs became the most vigorous sector of the Chinese economy in the 1980s and early 1990s. In 1978, before they were commandeered as socialist stalking horses of private enterprises, they employed an estimated 28 million people. In 1996 they employed 135 million. In some provinces such as Jiangsu and Shandong, they employed some 30 percent of the rural workforce.

Like the Xiaogang farmers, the TVEs were seen by Deng and the party leadership as manifestations of China's entrepreneurial spirit, as the red-hatted guards of economic reform, rather than disingenuous revisionists or tax evaders. "To cross the river," Deng used to say, "you have to feel the stones." The explosion of red hat businesses was not anticipated, still less mandated. "It was as if a strange army appeared in the countryside making and selling a huge variety of products," Deng said later. "This is not the achievement of our central government. This wasn't something I thought of. This was a surprise."

In retrospect, it is easy to see red hat companies as transitional forms: the vigorous, varied, multitudinous, early expressions of a long-frustrated entrepreneurial energy unleashed after decades of suppression. They were not mature forms of Chinese enterprise, any more than the cygnet is the mature form of the swan. The TVEs came under severe pressure during the economic recession of 1995–96. Many—30 percent according to some estimates—went out of business, and their previously privileged position straddling the public and private sectors was progressively undermined by the drastic public sector reforms and mass privatizations of SOEs in the late 1990s.

By then they had done their job. While the SEZs were sucking in an impressive amount of foreign investment and developing what was to become an enormous Chinese export business, the red hat firms were spreading the entrepreneurial word through rural China, and laying down the foundations of a market economy.

But Deng's quest for true socialism, using socialism's traditional antithesis, capitalism, to unleash "productive forces," was not all plain sailing.

Setbacks

Changes in the way the still-dominant SOEs were run reduced state revenues at a time when state investment and lending to businesses were rising. This situation became critical when, after reaching a peak in 1984, farm production fell and the state had to spend more to maintain food prices at levels prescribed in China's economic plan. Price controls at a time of shortage always create arbitrage opportunities, and China's merchants were not slow to exploit them. Individuals and SOEs bought food and other goods at planned prices and then sold them on at twice planned prices on the black market.

Deng realised that the party had stubbed its toe on a stone in the river; that price controls did not work in the socialist-capitalist hybrid system the country was developing, and would have to go. But he had reckoned without the power of expectations in free markets. By announcing the decision prematurely, he precipitated a frenzy of panic buying and hoarding. Prices were hastily liberalized, but by then supplies of food and other staples were so short that inflation rocketed. Price controls were reimposed at the end of 1988,

Deng's influence waned, and hard-liners introduced austerity measures.

From an economic point of view, the civil unrest that broke out in 1989 could scarcely have come at a better time. The people were so shocked by the violence, and by the simultaneous implosion of the once-revered Soviet Union, that the austerity measures, including a wage freeze, a two-thirds cut in state lending, and tight monetary policy, were accepted with barely a murmur of dissent.

The medicine worked. Farm production recovered, inflation eased as a consequence, and price controls were quietly relaxed.

The unrest was ostensibly about demands for multi-party democracy, and was billed as such by western media. But there was more to it than that. It attracted support among workers and peasants as well as students and the intellectual elite, because it served to focus the frustrations of ordinary people. After the first fine fiat of growth in the initial opening-up decade, the economic situation for workers had begun to deteriorate in the late 1980s.

Deng Xiaoping, in his mid-80s now but still adept politically, and with an acute sense of the way that winds were blowing, understood this. He saw in the students' demands for a "fifth modernization" (democracy), the violence in Beijing and similar demonstrations in other cities, such as Shanghai and Guangzhou, another "stone under the water."

There was discontent in the factories, and on the farms. It seemed clear to Deng that something had to be done.

Deng's southern tour

In early 1992 Deng boarded a special train and embarked on what is now known as his "southern tour" (*Nan Xun*), a four-day trip to the areas where his economic reforms had had the most impact.

Deng arrived at Shenzhen's brand-new station in January 1992, and explained his mission. The reform process was stalling and must be reignited. "If the economy cannot be boosted," he warned, "[it] will only lead to the collapse and disintegration of the Communist Party." He insisted that there was no conflict between making money and socialism, and urged local officials to push reforms and not act like "a woman with bound feet." (This was a reference to binding the feet of girls, often causing deformities, a practice common in China from the tenth to the twentieth centuries. The practice was prohibited by the PRC in 1949.)

Shenzhen itself also spoke eloquently of the benefit of reform and of SEZ status. In the first decade of the American experiment its economy had grown at 50 percent a year, and by 1991 it was generating $3.5 billion worth of output each year. The builders of Shenzhen's skyscrapers, who could reputedly complete three floors a day, were modern urban heroes.

The message to local officials was clear. Get with the program, and your town or village, however humble today, could be like Shenzhen within a decade. Perhaps the most important result of the tour was the confidence it gave to entrepreneurs such as Ye Maozhong (see page 17) and Feng Jun (see page 114), both of whom trace the origins of their entrepreneurial careers back to Deng's *Nan Xun*, to set up their own businesses.

As a political swansong – Deng died in 1997 at the age of 92 – the southern tour was a triumph. In October of 1992 the National Party Congress declared China a "socialist market economy," and wannabe Shenzhens began sprouting up like weeds in a hot summer. When Deng boarded his special train there were just 100 SEZs. By the end of the year there were 8,700 and counting. The SEZ Office had planned to organize SEZ development on "three alongs" – along the coast, along the Yangtze, and along China's border in the north-east. But provincial governments all over China took no notice and announced their own zones. Investment in the stock market and property boomed. The American experiment was back on track.

Privatization

The most conspicuous economic development during the second decade of China's American experiment had a hint of Britishness about it.

The main protagonist was Zhu Rhongji, deputy prime minister from 1993 to 1998 and prime minister from 1998 to 2003. Zhu's favourite occidental politician was Margaret Thatcher, prime minister of the United Kingdom from 1979 to 1990. Like Thatcher, Zhu was concerned with economic efficiency and competitiveness, and he

Box 1.2 Ye Maozhong

Chairman of Ye Maozhong Marketing (YMM)

Ye Maozhong with Mao Zedong
Source: Ye Maozhong Marketing

When Ye Maozhong finally leaves the company he founded, his spirit will linger, in the form of a hat. The hat, to Ye, is as important as the moustache was to Salvador Dali. He is never seen without it. It is part of his personal brand, just as his personal brand is an essential part of Ye Maozhong Marketing's corporate brand.

When I met the man beneath the hat in his stylish Shanghai office he was deploying his personal brand to dazzle a new YMM client, at a contract signing. YMM had not pitched for the business and had not negotiated fees. It never does. "If you trust us, come to us," YMM says. Many small and medium-sized Chinese companies do both.

Ye says YMM has prospered because it has grown up with the Chinese private entrepreneurs, understands their needs, and provides a one-stop marketing service including advertising, design, and marketing strategy consultancy. "Chinese domestic enterprises don't have the budget or the time to employ several different professional firms," he says. "They want one firm to solve all their problems. And they don't care much how we do it, as long as we deliver results."

So far as Ye knows, none of the founders of the successful Chinese advertising agencies have worked for international agencies, just as few Chinese entrepreneurs (YMM's main client base) have worked for international companies. "Most of the second generation have been educated in the West," he says, "but they are not simply doing what they have learned in business school. They are exploring ways to adapt international methods to local circumstances."

About 3 percent of YMM's clients are international firms. Most multinationals use international agencies in China, because they sign for the worldwide business. In Ye's view that is a mistake. It makes sense for multinationals to use western firms outside China, but everything is so different in China, in such areas as marketing environment, culture, consumer behavior, characteristics of media, and local regulations, that international firms lack the knowledge and resources to handle it all. That is why many well-known global marketing companies operate less integrated businesses in China.

Ye worked with the consumer goods giant Procter & Gamble for three years, helping it to promote its products in rural markets. He learned a lot about how to become more professional, and so agrees that not all you learn at western business school is useless. The problem is how to put what you learn into practice in China. He says the emphasis of international firms on their own cultures and systems is not conducive to staff development.

"If you ask people about the Chinese model," he says, "most of them will say it's not yet established, that we're still experimenting. But that's the beauty of exploration. You can still create."

Ye started his firm accidentally in 1995, when marketing was still in its infancy in China. He was a television editor, and was asked to edit a television commercial. He realized he was born for the industry. It was a struggle at first, but he understood his clients, made some famous commercials, and became famous himself. He says clients are not good at marketing themselves. He helps them with that, and offers a more personal service; he teaches them how to spend their money wisely, to appreciate and collect art, invest in real estate, and expand their horizons with travel. It is part of Ye's one-stop-shop marketing approach. In a culture that frowns on bragging, it is hard for people to feel comfortable promoting them-selves. Ye tells them that in promoting themselves, they are promoting the company.

People say that if China had a Philip Kotler – the leading western marketing guru – it would be Ye Maozhong.

He sees his adult life as falling into three parts: first, working for a living in television; second, starting YMM and making money; third, which is the current phase, having made his fortune, giving something back. He feels he is carrying people's expectations. He has started two schools of marketing, he writes books, runs a very popular blog, and has a personal web page on which "the hat" looms large.

It's an army hat. He was very moved by the story of the Long March when he was a boy and he is a great admirer of Mao Zedong, of whom there is a statue in his garden. "I have carried out Mao's thoughts without thinking," he says.

Luyang Jiang

saw in China's huge state-owned sector a target ripe for the plucking.

Although China remained, for a long time, ideologically opposed to the idea of "privatization," a policy known as *zhuada fangxiao* (keep the large, release the small) led to the sale or closure of huge numbers of China's smaller SOEs and COEs (collectively owned enterprises) at an enormous price in jobs. According to official statistics, the share of industrial output and urban employment accounted for by SOEs and COEs fell from 76 percent and 76 percent respectively in 1980, to 28 percent and 44 percent respectively in 1998.

But privatization was not a matter of principle, as it was for the Thatcher government in the United Kingdom. China still has a large state-owned sector and some very large "central SOEs." The policy was inspired not by an ideology that saw SOEs as incorrigibly inefficient, but by a recognition that a strong modern economy required a large and vigorous private sector. In pursuing privatization Zhu also had in mind the fact that, since 1986, China had been negotiating to join the World Trade Organization (WTO), and that WTO members favoured a "mixed" economy with a good blend of private and state ownership.

China's accession to the WTO, on December 11, 2001 (after 15 years of negotiation), was a major step in the integration of China with the world economy. It heralded a period of rapid economic growth, and was strong corroboration of the wisdom of the decision in 1978 to embark on China's American experiment.

In retrospect, it can be seen that the experiment succeeded for 30 years because of an improbable combination of a strong government, with a clear sense of direction, pursuing what, in the early years at least, was a liberal industrial policy. This was the "hardware" of China's economic miracle; the context within which the hitherto latent entrepreneurial energies of China's merchant classes became dedicated to the realization of the American Dream.

The "software" was supplied by a process of acculturation. China's educated urban elite were encouraged to learn English – the *lingua franca* of business – start their own companies, consume, and above all travel, particularly to the home of the dream, America.

It was this software that brought the two countries together. When the experiment started in 1978, China and America were poles apart in practically every respect, except for the belief they shared in the vital importance of entrepreneurs. By 2008, the American Dream was all but realized for some, and had become close enough to touch for the rest of China's so-called "300 million Americans," people who had learned English, and adopted American business manners and management styles.

It seemed, to some outsiders, that China's American experiment was about to end in victory for the merchants over the administrators, and what amounted to the economic fusion of the two countries.

But the administrators, in the form of the CCP, had always been in control. The Party had opened its doors to private business people at its 2002 National Congress (not to be confused with the annual National People's Congress), and 3 million merchants had joined the party before the next National Party Congress in 2007, after a law allowing private property was passed. But the influx of 3 million merchants into a party with over 70 million members did not weaken the power of the administrators.

Four corporate species

The overlaying of the American way of doing business, on a merchant culture that had gone through dramatic changes over the previous century or so, was bound to generate an unusually varied range of businesses and enterprises. Four distinct types of modern Chinese enterprise can be identified.

State-owned enterprises (SOEs)

Following Zhu Rhongji's *keep the large, release the small* brand of privatization, most of China's SOEs are either large or very large. They dominate such sectors as oil and gas, utilities, metals, car manu- facturing, chemicals, telecommunications, and banking. China's "central SOEs" have been owned by the State Assets Supervision and Administration Commission (SASAC) since 2003. At time of writing (May 2010) there were 126 central SOEs, and a new asset manage- ment company, Guoxin Asset Management Corp., had been set up to acquire smaller SOEs, and help the SASAC reach its goal of cutting central SOE numbers to 100 by the end of 2010 and to 80 eventually. CEO positions at SOEs are political appointments, and SOE managers are obliged to follow SASAC rules in many key management areas. SOEs have some of the attributes of large private sector companies, but they are not free to experiment with and develop new management approaches or styles. Their ethos is closer to the administrator's than to the merchant's. According to official figures SOEs account for 3 percent of domestic enterprises, but 30 percent of assets.

Small and medium-sized enterprises (SMEs)

Many of China's SMEs have developed from the TVEs through which Chinese entrepreneurialism was expressed in the early years after the opening up in 1978 (see above). Most are family businesses run by dictatorial patriarchs or matriarchs, with limited ambitions to grow, or expand beyond their local bases. As specialist suppliers and sub-contractors, they constitute an important part of China's manufacturing base, but they are not and have no wish to be at the forefront of management or organizational development. In its 2009 SMEs report, the China National Development and Reform Commission estimated that small enterprises with annual sales of less than 30 million yuan accounted for 90 percent of companies, and 36 percent of national output, and that medium-sized enterprises, with annual sales of 30–300 million yuan, accounted for 9 percent of companies and 29 percent of national output.

Large private enterprises (western clones)

These are private sector companies, started by ambitious so-called "sea-turtles"—ethnic Chinese returning home after long absences—who have taken MBA courses at western business schools, worked for western firms and are steeped in western management thinking. They see themselves as "professional," and bringing "professionalism," by which they mean the tools, techniques, and approaches of western management, which they see as a valuable competitive advantage in China's still relatively "amateurish" private sector, is often an important part of their business idea. Many CEOs of such firms see themselves as leading-edge players in the development of Chinese management, because they are making it more "professional," and, by casting their companies in the western mould, they are making them globally competitive. Such "West is best" CEOs can be divided into two groups: high-tech entrepreneurs trained on the west coast of America, and more financially oriented entrepreneurs schooled on the east coast of America. Let's call them "clones."

Large private enterprises (New China)

These are private sector companies, started by entrepreneurs, some of whom are "sea-turtles" trained in the West, but all of whom are, or have become, skeptical about the applicability of western-style management to Chinese companies and markets. They are reaching back to their cultural roots for ideas, principles, concepts, and tools for thought to replace or combine with features of other models of management. In the process these entrepreneurs are developing, for the most part unconsciously, a new and distinctively Chinese style or model of management. Let's call them "New China" enterprises.

Table 1.1 summarizes, in a rough and conceptual way, the influences on the management styles employed in the four types of enterprise of three elements: western management, what might be called the "administrator ethos," and, for want of a better term, the "spirit of China."

Table 1.1 Type of enterprise and influence on management style

Enterprise type	Estimated level of influence		
	Western	Administrator ethos	Spirit of China
SOEs	Low/medium	Very high	Medium/high
SMEs	Low to high	Low	High to low
Clones	Medium/high	Low	Low/medium
New China	Low/medium	Low/medium	High/very high

As indicated in the table, SME management styles embrace the whole range, from entirely western to entirely spirit of China. It is only after enterprises grow out of the SME category that they split into the "clone" and "new China" categories, and signs of a new kind of management in the latter category become visible.

This new management style emerging from an as yet relatively minor segment of Chinese business, characterized here as "New China," is the main focus of this book. It is emerging, partly from a growing disenchantment with the western management model that began before the 2007–08 global financial crisis, but deepened afterwards, and partly from the success and the growing self-confidence of some of China's private entrepreneurs.

Although most visible in the "New China" companies, the "spirit of China" component is growing in importance in all four categories, fostered by scholars, think tanks, the government, and the Chinese media. When you ask any senior media figure or academic about it, their eyes light up and enthusiastic conversations follow. It's in the air. It's big. It's coming. It's like 1978 all over again.

The reason that the emergence of this new approach to management in China has so far gone undetected by western observers is that when they study China's corporate sector, they tend to focus on China's large SOEs and foreign-owned Chinese firms (some of the leaders of which are aware that something new is emerging), and seldom talk to New China entrepreneurs.

Profiles of ten New China entrepreneurs, interviewed by the author and Luyang Jiang, are scattered throughout this book to illustrate the kind of thinking that is going on in their minds as they try to develop a management style and way of doing business that are better suited to China's business environment than the western way.

Cultural incompatibility

It is helpful to distinguish between, on the one hand, the economic ties that link China to the United States, which have become steadily closer (particularly since China joined the WTO, and westerners began to talk about the emergence of a new "G2"), and on the other hand, the cultural and social coming together of the two countries as a consequence of China's pursuit of the American Dream. The economic ties will become closer still as business globalization progresses and world trade expands, but the cultural and social convergence, which, in the major cities at any rate, has been equally rapid for most of the past 30 years, may be approaching some kind of limit.

A limit or barrier of this kind was always going to appear at some stage. When Deng Xiaoping said that "When our thousands of Chinese students abroad return home, you will see how China will transform itself," he had in mind economic, not cultural transformation. The sea-turtles could only ever have been ambassadors for the American way of business.

The culture associated with the American Dream helped to foster an aspirational outlook and hunger for material wealth among China's "300 million Americans." But 300 million Americans, about as many as live in the United States, were never going to be enough in China to effect a cultural transformation. The ancient Chinese culture is much too strong, runs much too deep, and its home is in the country, not the cities. This became very clear in 2008.

Summary

- Deng Xiaoping's opening up in 1978 introduced economic liberalism to China.
- The chosen model of economic development was the American model.
- The de-collectivization of farming led to a spontaneous upsurge of entrepreneurialism.
- When economic progress faltered in the late 1980s Deng's "southern tour" reinvigorated the reform process.
- Privatization of SOEs, and China's accession to the WTO in 2001, provided additional stimuli.
- The overlay of the American business culture on China's merchant tradition and the legacy of communism created four main types of Chinese company.
- Although China grew steadily closer to the United States economically, there were limits to the associated cultural convergence.

Note

1 *China Rises. How China's Astonishing Growth Will Change the World*, by John Farndon, Virgin Books, 2007, is an important source for this section and China's post-1978 industrialization.

CHAPTER 2

2008, the turning point

On May 12, 2008 at 2.28 pm local time a major earthquake, measuring 8.0 on the Richter scale, hit China's Sichuan province. According to official figures issued on July 21, 2008, almost 70,000 people were confirmed dead, 375,000 were injured, over 18,000 were listed as missing and 4.8 million were made homeless.

The earthquake, also known as the Wenchuan earthquake, because its epicentre was in Wenchuan county, some 80 kilometers northwest of Chengdu, the capital of Sichuan, was stronger but less deadly than the Tangshan earthquake in July 1976, which was estimated to have led to the deaths of 240,000 people. There were other differences too.

In an eventful year for China – known as the "Curse of 1976" – the Tangshan quake followed the death of China's President Zhou Enlai in January, and preceded the death of Mao Zedong in September, and the arrest of the "Gang of Four" in October.

On the day of the quake on July 28, the Gang of Four, led by Mao's wife (soon to be widow) Jiang Qing, were still in power and seemed more concerned with their battle against "rightist deviationists" in general, and Deng Xiaoping in particular, than with organizing disaster relief.

Hua Guofeng, Mao's successor as paramount leader, gained political prestige by expressing concern and visiting Tangshan on August 4, a week after the quake, to survey the damage. Two months later he effected what amounted to a *coup d'état*, by ordering the arrest of the Gang of Four.

Another feature of the Tangshan quake and its aftermath is that it was an entirely internal affair. No requests for foreign help were issued, and very little information about the earthquake itself or subsequent relief efforts was released.

In 2008, Premier Wen Jiabao took the first available flight to the Sichuan disaster area. He was there within hours. He wept for the dead, comforted the injured and talked to the families of victims. "I am Grandpa Wen," he called to trapped school children. "You will be rescued." He was shown on television clambering over the rubble and shrugging off assistance when he fell and injured his arm. One correspondent to the *People's Daily* website expressed the general reaction: "From the disaster site, the familiar and resolute voice made the victims calm. The 65-year-old man helped us to weep. This is our Government, this is our Premier Wen whose heart is entwined with ours."

The day after the earthquake the Chinese government announced that it would gratefully accept international help. Rescue teams from South Korea, Japan, Singapore, and Russia arrived a few days later. The United States made satellite images of the quake areas available to the Chinese authorities, and over the weekend, two US Air Force C-17s landed at Chengdu with tents and generators. But although welcome, international assistance was not vital. China licked her own wounds, quickly and efficiently.

The government's disaster management attracted plaudits throughout the world. Francis Marcus, of the International Federation of the Red Cross, described China's rescue program as "swift and very efficient." The *Economist* praised China for reacting "rapidly and with uncharacteristic openness," and several western commentators compared China's handling of the Sichuan quake favorably with the Myanmar (Burma) government's secretive response to Cyclone Nargis, which had devastated that country 10 days earlier, and China's own handling of the Tangshan quake in 1976.

There was praise at home, too. China's press and media coverage of the aftermath of the quake led a professor at Peking University to comment: "This is the first time the Chinese media has lived up to international standards." He felt the press had fulfilled a vital function after the earthquake by helping the Chinese people to see and appreciate the scale of the disaster, and to share the pain. It was said to be the first time that the Chinese people were able to feel a sense of being one nation with a shared destiny. During and after the relief efforts, the government convened regular and frequent press conferences to brief the media on developments and progress. This was also a departure from normal practice, which is said to have reflected the realization of government and the media of the importance of transmitting the right messages after natural disasters.

More openness on the part of the government and an appreciation of how to use the media to project a positive image of the government have been lasting legacies of the Sichuan earthquake.

China's official news agency, Xinhua, established an online rescue request center to allow people to identify gaps or deficiencies in rescue efforts. When it became known that rescue helicopters were having trouble landing in the epicentre area in Wenchuan, a student proposed a new landing spot online, which was immediately adopted.

Volunteers set up several websites to hold contact information for victims and evacuees.

The State Council declared a three-day period of national mourning for the quake victims. The National Flag and the regional flags of Hong Kong and Macau were flown at half mast. It was the first time a period of national mourning had been declared for an event other than the death of a state leader. A the end of the three days at 2.28 pm, May 19, exactly one week after the earthquake, China stood in silence for three minutes while police and fire sirens, and the horns of vehicles, ships, and trains, sounded. The silence ended in a spontaneous burst of cheering in Tian'anmen Square, and cries of *"China jiayou"* (long live China) and *"Sichuan jiayou."*

The Ningbo Organizing Committee of the Beijing Olympic torch relay suspended the relay during the mourning period, Macau casinos were closed, and servers for online computer games were shut down.

China's Ministry of Civil Affairs reported that within two days of the quake, the Chinese public had donated 10.7 billion yuan (about US$1.5 billion) to help earthquake victims. Booths for donations were set up in schools, banks, and petrol stations throughout China, and long queues of people waiting to give blood formed in most of

China's major cities. Many people donated through text messages on mobile phones to accounts set up by China Unicom and China Mobile.

The *China Youth Daily* estimated that about 200,000 volunteers from all over China flocked to the earthquake zone. Beef was trucked in from Inner Mongolia, sleeping bags were brought from Shenzhen, and building material came from Chongqing. Several millions of bottles of water and packets of noodles were donated by the public. People watched television news to see what to bring. Others learned from their first visits what was needed and then made repeated trips to the stricken areas.

Young volunteers from the cities comforted the bereaved and helped survivors to salvage their belongings. Doctors from Shanghai flew to Chengdu, and hiked into remote areas to offer emergency medical assistance. Convoys of private cars bringing food, cooking oil, and cell phones donated by businesses clogged the mountain roads. Huge piles of donated clothes were a common symbol of public generosity and concern in local towns.

Houston Rockets center Yao Ming, one of China's most popular sports stars, gave $214,000, and another $71,000 to the Red Cross Society of China, which, by May 14, had received a total of $26 million in donations.

On May 15, *United Daily News* reported that mainland China's top 10 richest people had donated over 32.5 million yuan (US$4.6 million) by May 13; not nearly enough, according to Chinese internet users.

On the evening of May 18, CCTV-1 broadcast a four-hour charity gala called *The Giving of Love* hosted by CCTV regulars, and attended by celebrities from the worlds of entertainment, literature, business, and politics. Donations during the evening amounted to 1.5 billion yuan (US$208 million).

On May 24, Hong Kong film star Jackie Chan donated $1.57 million to the earthquake victims and said he wanted to make a film about the disaster. A few days later the Sichuan Earthquake Disaster Relief Command was set up in Chengdu by the Chinese action star Jet Li's One Foundation, a charity he had set up to help victims of natural disasters. Li said One Foundation's post-disaster work would focus on the elderly, orphans, and the disabled.

On May 23, China's commerce minister, Chen Deming, thanked foreign companies for their earthquake donations and rejected criticism on Chinese websites that they were "international misers" and failing to do enough. He said China had had "strong support" from foreign companies, and that they had given by then 1.95 billion yuan (about US$280 million) in cash and supplies.

Chinese websites put enormous pressure on private companies, local and foreign, to give generously. Those that did not were accused of being "iron roosters," too stingy to shed one feather. Wang Shi, a Chinese real estate developer, was pilloried for only giving what the websites judged a paltry $290,000. In the end, Wang gave about $30 million and admitted the bad publicity had negatively affected his company's stock price.

It was estimated that private companies eventually gave a total of over $1 billion. Wealthy individuals and successful companies have begun to pay more attention to their public images following the earthquake, and the western idea of corporate social responsibility (CSR) has been introduced to China.

Outsiders were surprised by the spontaneous outburst of generosity and concern, the eagerness with which ordinary Chinese people took the initiative, and the flexibility and openness of the government in allowing them to do so. One Chinese political analyst expressed the view in the *Los Angeles Times* that the Chinese government was "changing its ruling ideology to become more people-oriented." A western diplomat told *The Times* of London that the Chinese people had "been worrying about the selfishness of their society obsessed with making money," and were now "rejoicing that in their new-found prosperity they can afford to be altruistic."

Jiang Xipei, founder and chairman of the Far East group (electrical cables, medicines, real estate, and investment), exemplifies, in his concern for disabled people, the new sense of social responsibility among China's business elite (see page 31).

Because most Chinese people still have very little of it, money is still closely associated with happiness and success in China. As Patrick Mattimore pointed out in an article in *Global Times*,[1] in a Reuters-Ipsos opinion survey of 23 countries in February 2010, two-thirds of

Box 2.1 Jiang Xipei

Chairman of Far East

Jiang Xipei
Source: Far East

The first thing you notice about Jiang Xipei, founder and chairman of electrical cables, medicines, real estate, and investment group Far East, is his use of the word "we," rather than the more usual entrepreneurial "I," when he talks about his company. He owned all of the shares initially, but says "every partner and employee has contributed to the development of the company." Management and the employees currently own all the shares.

In the early years Jiang was a factory worker, and head of marketing and finance too. As a former watch-maker he was good with machines and knew how to sell products at a profit. But as the company grew and it became impossible to take care of everything, he initiated a system of weekly meetings. Now that Jiang has assembled a strong management team working with a good management system, the meetings are quarterly. He sets much store by systems. Nothing should be done before standards and systems are established, he says.

The time Jiang spends on day-to-day management has declined, along with his shareholding, which has been given to key members of the company. These days, he spends part of his time reading and studying for training courses, part on long-term planning and personnel issues, and part on public relations. He also finds time to work for disabled people. About a quarter of Far East's 6,200 or so employees are disabled, and Jiang has set up a special fund to help other disabled people get training, and find jobs. He sees it as part of "giving back," as many successful Chinese entrepreneurs put it, to society, and to China.

Now that his company has developed to a point where it can operate efficiently without his full-time attention, Jiang is becoming the Confucian ideal of a *junzi* (morally correct person).

The group's four divisions (cables, medicines, real estate, and investment) are owned by a holding company. Investment decisions are made by an investment committee over which Jiang presides, but each division is run by a general manager.

In addition to his own E-MBA courses, Jiang also provides training for his employees. Every employee has at least a month's training a year, and middle managers get two months. Far East was among the first Chinese companies to set up its own corporate university.

Far East began in a small village. Its subsequent success has made its tax payments so important to the local economy that the local government has asked Jiang to become a special adviser. He intends to represent local entrepreneurs, and to convince local government officials to improve the business environment, by liberalizing the market further, to promote social development.

Jiang has had his problems with illiberal markets. When he started to design and make electrical cable in 1990 he did not sell any for six months, because he had no familiar brand and no quality certificate, and the state-owned trading outlets through which electrical cable was normally sold were reluctant to stock his brand. Business improved after a while, but not quickly enough for Jiang. In a classic, mold-breaking entrepreneurial move, he decided to open his own franchised stores opposite the state-owned outlets. He opened five stores in the first year and sold cable worth 4.6 million yuan. In the second year he began to attract customers from the state-owned outlets, and turnover reached 18 million yuan with 28 employees. He was the first in the industry to use the franchise model, in which franchisees share profits with Far East, and even more shocking for the state-owned trading outlets, the first to state his prices in television and newspaper advertisements.

The next step in 1991 was to develop a sales management system, to link the income of sales staff to their sales volume and performance. As the store network expanded, it became harder for headquarters to keep an eye on it all, so Jiang set up an independent auditing department that same year, to ensure standard and transparent sales reporting.

"When I do things" says Jiang, "I don't keep my team in the dark. I make sure they clearly understand the objectives. I look for like-minded partners. This is not my company. They should not think they're only working for me or that Far East has nothing to do with them." The company culture he articulated 15 years ago is based on the Chinese characters *he* and *ling*. *He* is worth, or value, and means harmony and peace. *Ling* is the method, and means flexibility. Jiang discusses this idea constantly with employees, encourages them to identify with it, criticizes any behavior that contradicts it, and says his behavior should "embody the idea."

Luyang Jiang and the author

the Chinese people surveyed believed that money is "the best sign of a person's success." This was higher than in any other country apart from South Korea, and twice as high as in the United States.

But thanks partly to the emotions unleashed by the television pictures of the Sichuan earthquake victims, questions are being asked in China about fairness and the relationship between money and happiness. In an online chat with web users on February 27, 2010, Premier Wen emphasized the government's responsibility to bring about greater distributive justice. "Distributing the cake of social wealth," Wen said "is a matter of being just and fair to everybody."

The Communist Party held the reins of power in China in 2008 as it had done at the time of the Tangshan earthquake in 1976. But this was a different country, a different people: more open, more self-assured, more opinionated, and more socially conscious. It was less equal to be sure, but far more prosperous. And the people who had prospered particularly were more conscious of the responsibilities that came with their wealth. In the three decades between the two great earthquakes China changed culturally and socially as well as economically. Economic success was leading to "what next?" and "where do we go from here?" questions.

This was not "communism" as the rest of the world knew it. To use Deng's metaphor, it was a cat of a different color. It was a China the West had to try to understand all over again, not as a twentieth-century neo-communist state, purged of its history by the Cultural Revolution, but as the modern manifestation of a great and ancient civilization.

By 2008 there were many more signs that a new country had risen in the east, different from the China of Mao Zedong, but increasingly similar in many ways to, although distinct from, other countries of the developed world.

The Beijing Olympics

On July 13, 2001, just five months before China's accession to the World Trade Organization (WTO) on December 11, 2001, the International Olympic Committee (IOC) appointed Beijing host city for the 2008 Summer Olympic Games in preference to Toronto, Paris, Istanbul, and Osaka. China became the 18th nation to host a Summer Olympics. It was a welcome recompense for China's disappointment eight years earlier when Beijing had led all but the final round of IOC voting for the 2000 Summer Olympics, only to lose to Sydney by two votes.

The games opened on August 8, 2008, three months after the Sichuan earthquake, for which they represented, for many Chinese people, a poignant but positive counterpoint. The games ended on August 24, having achieved the largest television audience ratings in Olympic history.

China invested heavily in the Beijing Olympics with new facilities and transport systems. Of the 37 venues used to host the events, 12 were built specifically for the Olympics. The games were generally recognized by the world's media to have been a logistical success, the facilities were widely admired, and the fact that contrary to the expectations of some, they were finished on time, was seen as further evidence of China's world-class project management ability, which had been displayed earlier that year during the earthquake relief efforts. Fears ahead of the games of terrorist attacks were not realized; no athletes protested on the podium; and the air quality in Beijing, about which some had expressed concerns, proved acceptable, if not exemplary.

The success of the Olympics as an international event was a source of considerable pride in China, amplified by the good performances of China's own Olympians. As usual, the United States led the medals table, with a total of 110, but China was a close second with 100, and won many more gold medals (51) than the United States (36).

China's space program

The origins of China's space program date back to the formation of the Fifth Academy of the Defense Ministry, in 1956. Its director was Qian Xueshen, recently deported from the United States because he was a communist, and its aim was to develop ballistic missiles to combat perceived threats from the United States and later the Soviet Union.

When the USSR launched *Sputnik 1* in 1957, Mao decided, at the 1958 National Party Congress, that China should become the equal of the two superpowers, and launched Project 581, to put a satellite into orbit by 1959 to celebrate the People's Republic of China's (PRC's) 10th anniversary.

By the time China exploded its first atom bomb on October 16, 1964, a medium-range ballistic missile (MRBM) program was bearing fruit, and an intercontinental ballistic missile (ICBM) program was being planned.

Development began on a submarine-launched ballistic missile system in 1967, and as the race to the Moon between the USSR and the United States approached its climax, Mao and Zhou Enlai decided the PRC must not be left behind, and launched China's own manned space program.

The pace of development slowed following Mao's death, but interest soon revived and an ambitious manned space program was proposed in 1986, consisting of manned spacecraft and space station projects. Although it came to nothing, parts of this program survived in the 1992 "Project 921."

After the Cold War and Deng's opening-up, the names used in China's space program, which had previously echoed China's revolutionary history, were replaced by more spiritual words. The old Long March rocket became the Divine Arrow, the space capsule was re-named the Divine Ship (*Shenzhou*) and the space plane was the Divine Dragon.

On November 20, 1999, 50 years after the PRC's birth, the *Shenzhou 1* spacecraft was launched and then recovered after a flight of 21 hours. Less than three years later, on October 15, 2003, Yang Liwei made his historic 21-hour flight in the *Shenzhou 5* spacecraft, and China became only the third country to send a human being into space in its own vehicle. This marked the completion of phase one of Project 921.

The second phase of Project 921 started with *Shenzhou 7*, the first space walk mission. It carried a complement of three "taikonauts," and was completed successfully in September 2008, one month after the end of the Olympic Games in Beijing. *Shenzhou 8*, an unmanned space laboratory module, *Shenzhou 9*, an unmanned cargo vehicle, and a manned *Shenzhou 10* were scheduled to dock in late 2010 to create the first element of a small orbital space laboratory complex. The third and final phase of Project 921 is a larger, permanent space station, manned by a permanent crew.

China's National Space Administration (CNSA) launched its unmanned Moon exploration project in February 2004. CNSA administrator Sun Laiyan said the project would involve three phases: orbiting the Moon, landing, and returning samples. The current plan seems to be to develop unmanned lunar orbiting and landing vehicles from 2012 to 2017, and then to embark on a manned Moon landing program. The Chinese have penciled in 2024 as the year of their first moonwalk.

There are as yet unofficial dreams of even greater grandeur. In May 2007 China's famed first astronaut, Yang Liwei, hinted at the 16th Human in Space Symposium held by the International Academy of Astronautics in Beijing that a lunar base was a necessary step towards a flight to Mars and the outer planets. There have been suggestions that a 20-year unmanned Mars exploration program could begin in 2014, and might be followed by a manned phase in 2040–60.

The US National Aeronautics and Space Administration (NASA), which still dwarfs CNSA in its size and accomplishments, also dreams of a manned Mars mission. But the Obama administration's decision in February 2010 to cancel Constellation, NASA's "back-to-the moon" program, makes it hard for devotees of space exploration to escape the suspicion that China will eventually take over from the United States the leadership baton for humanity's extraterrestrial adventure.

Attributes of power

If, as seems very unlikely, Deng Xiaoping had had a vision of what "good" would look like 30 years hence when, in 1978, he set China on its path to modernization, and if his vision had taken the form of a list of attributes and accomplishments of China in 2008, what might have been on it?

The four modernizations were of agriculture, industry, science and technology, and national defense. In very general terms Deng could be forgiven for a smile of satisfaction, had he known how it would turn out. China's agriculture and industry were in rude health in 2008, Chinese science and technology were thriving, as indicated by the success of the space program and the increasing sophistication of China's manufacturing sector, and China's military power was more than formidable enough in 2008 to face down any conceivable threat (see page 99).

With the horror of the Tangshan earthquake still fresh in his mind in

1978, Deng might have hoped that by 2008, China would have been much better equipped to bring succor to the victims of subsequent natural disasters. Here too, as China's very competent handling of the Sichuan earthquake demonstrated, Deng would have had reason to feel satisfied and proud of the Chinese people.

One of Deng's intentions when announcing the great opening in 1978 was to bring China in from the cold; to integrate the country with the global community of nations. The government's decision, during Deng's stewardship, to apply to join the WTO in 1986, reflected this intent. Had he lived to see it, Deng would have been pleased by China's accession to the WTO in 2001.

He might have experienced a twinge of satisfaction when China held its first Formula 1 motor racing Grand Prix in Shanghai in 2004, and was successful in its bid to host World Expo 2010 in Shanghai. It is certain he would have been delighted by the fact that Beijing hosted the 2008 Olympic Games, by the exceptional Chinese project management ability demonstrated by the organization of the games, and by the success of China's own Olympians in the competition for medals. The Olympic Games, perhaps more than any other achievement during the preceding 30 years, were the quintessential symbol of a China coming of age as a fully paid-up member of the modern world.

All in all, Deng would have felt that the American experiment had delivered the goods for China and its people. He might have been left with two nagging questions, however: "At what price?" and "What now?"

Collateral damage

Questions were being asked long before 2008 about the price China had paid, and was still paying, for the "goods" delivered by the American experiment and China's rapid economic development. Concerns currently preoccupying Chinese policy-makers can be grouped under four headings: inequality, unethical business practices, corruption, and pollution.

Inequality

Deng said that "To get rich is glorious," but he also said, "Young leading cadres have risen up by helicopter. They should really rise step by step." Scholars, academics, many business people, and party leaders became concerned that the pursuit of the American Dream had been taken too far; that the path it was taking China down was leading to a place that was not right for China; that a population of 1.3 billion needed a way of living and doing business that was not driven by the hunger for wealth, and was more in tune with the traditions and culture of China.

The growing inequality between China's rural poor, whose rise from near-destitution in 1978 had been "step by step," and the urban rich, who had "risen up by helicopter," was at odds with President Hu's expressed desire for a "harmonious society."

Before the opening-up in 1978, the state met the needs of all members of society, from the cradle to the grave. Child care, education, job placement, housing, health care, and care for the elderly were the responsibility of the individual's work unit, usually a state-owned enterprise or an agricultural commune. Remnants of this so-called "iron rice bowl" approach to welfare still survive in SOEs and some large private companies, but China's health care system was largely privatized in the 1990s. The transition from state to private provision was a transition from bad to worse, particularly for the rural poor. In 2007, the World Health Organization (WHO) ranked China's health system at 144th out of 190 countries in terms of quality and access.

The New Rural Co-operative Medical Care System (NRCMCS) was set up in 2005 to overhaul the system and make it more afford-able for the rural poor. Under the NRCMCS, the annual cost of medical cover was fixed at 50 yuan (US$7) per head, of which 20 yuan was paid by the central government, 20 yuan by the provin-cial government, and 10 yuan by the patient. By September, 2007 some 80 percent of China's rural population (about 685 million people) had signed up. The new system was tiered. If a patient went to a small local hospital or clinic, the scheme covered 70–80 percent of the bill. If they went to a county hospital, the percentage of cost covered fell to 60 percent. If specialist help was needed in a city hospital, rural patients had to foot 70 percent of the bill.

The NRCMS helped to narrow the yawning urban–rural health gap, but those living in remote villages still relied on poorly trained and ill-equipped "barefoot doctors."

At a session of the State Council, presided over by Prime Minister

Wen Jiabao, in January 2009 the government announced that a total of 850 billion yuan ($124 billion) would be spent between 2009 and 2011, "to provide basic medical security to all Chinese in urban and rural areas, improve the quality of medical services, and make medical services more accessible to, and affordable for ordinary people." State news agency Xinhua said the plan aimed to provide some form of medical insurance for 90 percent of the population by 2011. Those covered would receive an annual subsidy of 120 yuan as from 2010. Medicine would also be covered by the insurance. Xinhua explained that the "Growing public criticism of soaring medical fees, a lack of access to affordable medical services, poor doctor–patient relationship, and low medical insurance coverage had compelled the government to launch the new round of reforms."

A growth dividend was also expected. Commenting on the scheme, Bai Zhongen, head of the economics department at Tsinghua University's School of Economics and Management, said a survey by the school in 2007 on the effects of rural health insurance on consumption had "found that in government-sponsored health insurance areas, people are spending more."

During the National People's Congress (NPC) in March, 2009 Premier Wen announced that central government spending on social security would rise by 18 percent in 2009 to 293 billion yuan ($43 billion) and local governments would spend more on social security too. He also announced plans to provide old-age pensions for China's 130 million rural migrant workers, and ways to transfer them when rural workers moved from one region to another.

The government's evident intention to discharge its responsibility under Article 14 of the Chinese constitution, to develop a welfare system "corresponding to the level of economic development," is a challenge of epic proportions. According to a report by the China Development Research Foundation, a government think tank, "China has to invest 5.74 trillion yuan by 2020, in building an all-round social welfare system to enhance people's livelihoods," covering pensions, education, health care, housing, employment, and help for rural residents and migrant workers. The foundation's chairman, Wang Mengkui, said that such a system was essential to "solve the problem" of the imbalance between urban and rural areas, and among regions, and to benefit the whole population.

Business practices

There were also concerns about the ethical short-cuts some Chinese business people appeared willing to take in the pursuit of money.

In 2007 a number of recalls and import bans on products made in or imported from China, including petfood, toys, toothpaste, lipstick, and some seafoods, were imposed by the product safety institutions of the United States, Canada, the European Union, Australia, and New Zealand. In the petfood case, contamination with melamine—a chemical used in plastics and resins—was suspected. By increasing the nitrogen content of substances to which it is added, melamine makes them appear to contain more protein. The Chinese government explicitly banned the practice on April 26, 2007, but melamine and its apparent protein-boosting effects were also implicated in the Sanlu powdered milk scandal which broke on July 16, 2008, when 16 children who had been fed on infant formula produced by the Sanlu Group were diagnosed with kidney stones. The affair caused an uproar in China. Another 21 companies were implicated. At least six babies died and another 294,000 became seriously ill because of melamine contamination. This time, official displeasure was made abundantly clear when one executive involved was sentenced to death in January, 2009.

Another death, this time self-inflicted, occurred as a result of a product safety scandal in China's world-leading toy industry. In August 2007 the body of Zhang Shuhong, a 52-year-old businessman, was found hanging on the third floor of the Lee Der toy factory in Foshan, southern China, following a recall by the world's largest toy company, Mattel of the United States, of a million toys coated with toxic lead paint.

Lee Der was not the only Chinese company involved. Mattel recalled a total of 19 million toys made in China. Zhang was reported to have been more sinned against than sinning; a victim of fraudulent suppliers. Chinese regulators blamed an unnamed paint supplier, and promised those involved would be "severely" punished.

Official concerns about the damage inflicted on the reputations of China and its merchant class by these scandals were emphasized by the execution on July 10, 2007 of Zheng Xiaoyu, the former head of China's State Food and Drug Administration, for taking bribes and dereliction of duty following a series of drug safety scandals. On the day after the execution Xinhua published an extract from the judgment: "Zheng Xiaoyu's grave irresponsibility in pharmaceutical safety inspection and failure to conscientiously carry out his duties, seriously damaged the interests of the state and people." *China Daily* said the sentence reflected Beijing's resolve to drive out corruption and ensure consumer safety.

Corruption

The most conspicuous set-piece in the party's attack on corruption came two years later. In October, 2009 a series of trials began in the city of Chongqing on the Yangtze River following a two-year anti-corruption campaign by local party officials under Communist Party chief and Politburo member Bo Xilai. The trials were the culmination of an investigation involving over 9,000 suspects, and 1,544 arrests, including those of 19 suspected gang leaders, hundreds of gang members, and a number of allegedly corrupt police and other government and Communist Party officials, including six district police chiefs and the city's deputy police commissioner, Wen Qiang. Charges included murder, assault, and operating illegal coal mines.

On October 21 three of the defendants in the first round of trials were sentenced to death, three received suspended death sentences, and another 25 were jailed. Among the most conspicuous defendants was deputy police commissioner Wen's sister-in-law Xie Caiping, a 46-year-old alleged "ringleader" of Chongqing's gangsters. She was brought to trial on October 14, and sentenced to 18 years in prison for running a gang that operated illegal gambling dens, illegally imprisoned people, harbored drug users, ran protection rackets, and bribed police.

The Chinese people, riveted by coverage of the trials, stood up as one to applaud the dramatic victory over Chongqing's gangsters. It was seen as a demonstration of the government's determination to wipe out the cancer of corruption. It was thought to have improved the chances of the urbane and charismatic Bo Xilai being recalled to Beijing, and becoming a member of the ruling Politburo Standing Committee in the new government in 2012.

Pollution

With 20 percent of the world's population, but barely 7 percent of the world's total water resources, China will find it increasingly difficult to maintain adequate supplies of fresh water. World Bank estimates suggest mainland China's annual water resources per head are a quarter of the world's average, and that half of China's 617 large cities, including Beijing, have water deficits. Reliance on underground water in Northern China is causing ground-cracking and subsidence in some regions.

Moreover, much of China's water is heavily polluted, and much more so than was previously thought, according to an official survey of pollution sources published in February 2010. The survey found that 30.3 million metric tonnes of pollution was discharged into water in 2007, more than double the original estimate. The increase was partly due to the inclusion for the first time of wastewater run-off from farms, which is rich in fertilizers and pesticides.

Ma Jun (not to be confused with Ma Yun, also known as Jack Ma, the founder and CEO of Alibaba – see page 124), one of China's leading environmentalists, has been warning about China's water crisis for years. His 1999 book, *China's Water Crisis* (*Zhongguo shui weiji*), has been compared to Rachel Carson's *Silent Spring*. He is director of the Institute of Public and Environmental Affairs (IPE), which developed the China Water Pollution Map, the first public database of water pollution information in China.

Ma welcomed the report as "an important, first step to recognizing the problem," but was dismayed by the findings. "We believed we needed to cut our emissions in half, but today's data means a lot more work needs to be done," he said.

The report also showed that China is producing far more industrial waste than previously thought. Solid waste, such as particulates from mines and steel mills, amounted to 49.1 million tons in 2007, over three times the originally reported figure. This explains why air quality is so poor in some of China's cities. According to the WHO, the air in 50 or so Chinese cities carried up to seven times more particulates than the WHO's safe limit.

Zhang Lijun, vice minister for environment protection, said at the press conference launching the survey that the large increases in the official figures reflected more accurate measurements. But to the dismay of environmentalists, who attribute China's pollution partly to the fact that the performance of local officials and SOE leaders is measured in purely economic terms, he said the results will not be considered in annual performance reviews of government officials.

According to Carbon Monitoring for Action (CARMA), China accounted for 27.3 percent of world carbon dioxide (CO_2) emissions in 2009, against the United States's 24.7 percent and Europe's 16.4 percent. Foreign environmentalists who point accusatory fingers at China, however, should beware of doing China an injustice. One reason why China's carbon footprint is so high is that western countries have exported their emissions problem by outsourcing manufacturing to China.

It is not as if the government is unaware of, or unconcerned by, the problem. The 2007 census unveiled in February 2010 was the largest ever in China, involving 570,000 people, and a billion pieces of data from nearly 6 million sources of pollution, including factories, farms, homes, and pollution-treatment centers. It took more than two years to complete, and is scheduled to be repeated in 2020. Its findings were alarming, but they were published by the government, even so.

There is also more material evidence of the government's concern. China's $498 billion "economic stimulus" package in November, 2008 included plans to improve sewage and rubbish treatment facilities, accelerate forest planting programs where China already has a good record, and increase energy conservation initiatives and pollution control projects.

China's 11th five year plan (2006–10) included cutting energy usage per unit of output by 20 percent, reducing major pollutants by 10 percent, and increasing renewable energy's contribution to China's total energy consumption to 10 percent by 2010, and 15 percent by 2020. China is among the world's leading investors in renewable energy technology, and a major producer of wind turbines and solar panels. It is playing a part in the global effort to wean humanity from its addiction to carbon.

Crisis and opportunity

Growing inequality, unethical business practices, the degradation of the environment, and the cancer of corruption were being frequently seen, by 2008, as among a number of "bads" associated with China's eager pursuit of the American Dream. They were not endemic in the dream itself, of course. They were the consequences of the hungers the dream inspired in a country of over a billion people, and of the application of a model that had evolved in a culture a few centuries old to a culture that could trace its origins back a few millennia.

But it was one thing to diagnose the problem, and quite another to decide what to do about it. A 30-year-old program that has yielded such benefits is not easy to abandon. A whole generation has grown up within China's economic liberalism, and acquired the hungers and aspirations it encourages. The Chinese Communist Party (CCP) has proved adept at nudging and prodding the people in new directions, and towards new priorities, but although China's so-called "300 million Americans" account for only a quarter of the population, they include many well-connected members of the party, and are a formidable political force that the CCP leadership takes on at its peril.

Much has been made in the West in recent years of the emergence of an apparently more "hawkish" Chinese foreign policy, particularly towards the United States. Increasingly vocal Chinese objections to US arms sales to Taiwan, a less respectful attitude to other world leaders at international gatherings, such as the Copenhagen climate change summit, and a Soviet-style military parade bristling with missiles in Beijing in October 2009, to celebrate the PRC's 60th birthday, are all signs, it is alleged, of an emerging superpower flexing its muscles and preparing to strut more forcefully on the world stage.

Another way of interpreting these signs is to see them as designed primarily for internal, rather than external audiences, as part of a long and painstaking campaign to lift the spell of the American Dream and all things American that has held the Chinese people in thrall for three decades.

Nothing could have been more helpful for the Chinese leadership in this endeavor than the global financial crisis of 2007–08 and the fact that it was precipitated by unwise sub-prime mortgage lending in the United States. It revealed a potential for nightmares in the American Dream, where greed, folly, and the reckless pursuit of wealth could overwhelm liberal capitalism's automatic regulators, and bring the world's banking system to the brink of collapse.

Suggestions in China's official media that this American Dream was perhaps not all it was cracked up to be, that it led ultimately to rapacious individualism among a wealthy elite that took no account of ordinary people, and put the stability of the financial system in jeopardy, all became far more plausible after the crisis, and so helped to prepare the way for a change in direction.

The CCP seems to believe that China has gone as far as it is healthy to go down the US road; that it is time to pause and reflect on how to proceed. A complete root and branch eradication of things American is not practical, desirable, or even conceivable, but the Chinese leadership believe there needs to be some kind of decoupling, some distancing, some kind of awakening from the American Dream, to allow the Chinese people to develop their own dream.

Quite what this new Chinese dream will be is not yet clear—it is more a matter of moving away than of moving towards—but a misty vision beckons of a non-American future. This watershed in Chinese history is reminiscent of another great turning point, heralded by a famous document that begins:

> When in the Course of human events it becomes necessary for one people to dissolve the political bands which have connected them with another and to assume among the powers of the earth, the separate and equal station to which the Laws of Nature and of Nature's God entitle them, a decent respect to the opinions of mankind requires that they should declare the causes which impel them to the separation.

The American Declaration of Independence, July 4, 1776

We are dealing here with cultural, rather than political, bands and separation, and apart from what has already been written it is hard to say what causes impel the separation. It is clear, however, that China is waking up from the American Dream, and refusing the rest of the world's implicit invitation to take its place as a half of a new "G2," or fuse into a "Chimerika." It came very close, but as happens when two magnets of the same polarity approach each other, an invisible force intervened at the last moment, and prevented an apparently inevitable fusion.

China has its own mind, of which it has lately been reminded. It is not in the business any longer of following, copying, or emulating.

The empires, ideologies, and models to the West and East, exemplars and oppressors, have lost their authority and influence. There are no exemplars for China today; no societies, nations or systems to envy, or admire; no trail-blazers worth following; no destinations others have reached that China is reaching for. The American experiment is over. China knows now that it must find its own way.

Something is coming

In their search for a new Chinese way, the people of China are not starting from scratch. The American experiment has left many open questions that will need to be addressed. What to do about China's "300 million Americans"? What to do about China's farmers? How to solve the problem of growing inequality? What is the right balance between exports and domestic consumption? How can domestic demand be increased? Should China's development vision be based on a few megacities, or many large regional cities? Given the weaknesses of the western model revealed by the 2007–08 financial crisis, what additional regulations are needed? What more can or should be done to reduce pollution and combat climate change?

Some of these challenges are common to all countries in the second decade of the twenty-first century, but China will approach them in its own way, guided by its own traditions. It will settle on solutions and reach conclusions that will be distinctively Chinese. Foreigners who fail to understand this could be surprised and wrong-footed.

The Sichuan earthquake revealed more than the fragility of China's geology. The response to it in China surprised many foreigners. It suggested that something deep down in the bowels of China's history and culture had been awakened, and was rising to the surface. What it is, and how it will interact with and shape tomorrow's world, no one can say at this stage, but it is a powerful force, and what it does will be important for China, and for the rest of the world.

It will be vitally important for business people, because it seems possible that from it a distinctively Chinese style of management, and way of doing and organizing business, could emerge in China's private sector, which will differ in several important respects from the standard American model that has guided Chinese commercial and industrial development for the past 30 years.

Summary

- The handling of the Sichuan earthquake revealed a new China to the world.
- The Beijing Olympics and China's successful space program are evidence of China's growing abilities and maturity.
- The American experiment had delivered the economic goods.
- But there was collateral damage, too – inequality, unethical business practices, corruption, pollution.
- The global financial crisis facilitated the ending of the American experiment.
- China is going its own way.

Note

1 Patrick Mattimore, "Obsession with money won't make nation happy," *Global Times*, March 8, 2010.

PART II

Spirit, land, energy

CHAPTER 3

The origins of Chinese management

It is often, perhaps usually, assumed that there is only one model of management; that differences at any one time between national management models can all be explained by differences in maturity, or degrees of integration with the world economy, and will fade as global competition weeds out less effective styles, and management everywhere converges on the optimum model.

According to this argument, the optimum model is the western model, and China can therefore count itself fortunate that it adopted the western model when it embarked on its American experiment and sent its brightest and best merchants to learn about management at US business schools. This allowed China to leap-frog intermediate, sub-optimal models in the evolution of its management culture, and go straight to the optimum.

The trouble with this idea is that there is no evidence that the US model of management is the creature of a long evolutionary process of trial and error during which many other models have been tested and found wanting. On the contrary, a strong argument can be made for seeing the American style of management and the large, limited liability publicly listed joint stock company, which is its chosen vehicle, as the creatures not of an inexorable working-out of some natural economic law, but of an accident.

The fateful accident occurred in America on October 5, 1841 on the Western Railroad between Worcester and Albany. Some scheduler had blundered, and two passenger trains collided. A conductor and one passenger were killed, and 17 others were injured. Although hardly a disaster by modern standards, news of these first fatalities for the young railroad industry caused great alarm. The Massachusetts legislature launched an investigation and the Western appointed an internal committee of inquiry.

In its "Report on Avoiding Collisions and Governing Employees" the Western committee of inquiry proposed "the assignment of definite responsibilities for each phase of the company's business, drawing ... lines of authority and communication for the railroad's administration, maintenance and operation."

The distinguished business historian Alfred Chandler argued that the implementation of the committee's recommendations created "the first modern, carefully defined, internal organizational structure used by an American business enterprise," and "the first [company] ... to operate through a formal administrative structure, manned by full-time salaried managers."[1]

Chandler argued that the modern company, and the managerial system that came with it, was invoked by circumstances:

> The visible hand of management replaced the invisible hand of market forces where and when new technology and expanded markets permitted a historically unprecedented high volume and speed of materials through the processes of production and distribution. Modern business enterprise was thus the institutional response to the rapid pace of technological innovation and increasing consumer demand in the United States during the second half of the nineteenth century.

But suppose there had been no accident on the Western Railroad. It would probably not have occurred had the electric telegraph been introduced two years earlier than it was. Was the emergence of the modern company and the American system of management inevitable, or might the evolution of business organization and management have taken a different path, had that Western scheduler been more alert or been warned of the danger by telegraph?

The American management system did not emerge fully formed in the mid-nineteenth century. Its system of bureaucracy was inherited from the European monopoly-farming trading companies formed in the seventeenth and eighteenth centuries, which were more like private armies than business enterprises. And its hierarchical shape was based on the military class system, where power was concentrated at the top. It was this hierarchical shape, strengthened, after the implementation of the Western Railroad inquiry's recommendations by the addition of the divisional line-and-staff organization, that provided the context for the evolution of the American management model. It endowed the enterprise with a single guiding mind, the prime role of which was to formulate and orchestrate the implementation of strategy.

Chandler suggested that, by the outbreak of the American Civil War in 1861, the "modern American business enterprise" had been born:

> The needs of safety and then efficiency had led to the creation of a managerial hierarchy, whose duties were carefully defined in organizational manuals and charts. Middle and top managers supervised, coordinated, and evaluated the work of lower level managers who were directly responsible for the day-to-day operations.

Business schools

As Harvard Business School professor John Kotter pointed out, the new companies began complaining about shortages of qualified staff to run their organizations as early as the 1860s.[2] The University of Pennsylvania responded to this skill shortage in 1881 by founding the Wharton School of Finance and Commerce, which offered an undergraduate "management" degree. Similar schools were set up in California, Chicago, and elsewhere before the end of the nineteenth century. In 1908 the Harvard Business School (HBS) was founded to offer a Master's degree in business administration (MBA).

George Baker, head of what would become Citicorp, was impressed by the Harvard school, and in 1925 gave it the money to construct an eight-building campus. The following year 58,000 students, taught by 2,500 faculty at 132 American schools, majored in business. Most of them joined large companies.

It was inevitable, given the inspirations for the schools, and the destinations of their graduates, that intimate relationships would develop between the "B-schools," as they are now known, and large companies. This was particularly true at HBS. The library is named after George Baker, the MBA classrooms are Aldrich and Rockefeller (Standard Oil), the dining hall is Kresge (K-Mart), the executive programs are taught in Cumnock (J. P. Stevens), and the main office building is Morgan (Morgan Guaranty and Stanley).

The US business schools played a vital role in the evolution of managerial capitalism, and of the American management style, by providing the skills Chandler's new enterprises needed to perfect the system of administrative coordination. They were the officers' training colleges for large companies. HBS was and remains to big business what West Point is to the US Army.

By becoming the main repositories of management knowledge, and world-leading laboratories for the advancement of the management sciences, the American B-schools have helped promote the idea that American management thinking was "leading edge," and the American management style, which the B-schools are constantly refining, was the optimum style towards which all other styles are converging.

The truth is that the origins of the American management model lie in the accidental birth of one particular kind of organization in America in the mid-nineteenth century, to the service of which it was and continues to be dedicated, and within the cultural, political, industrial, and economic environments prevailing in the United States at that time. There is no reason to suppose that it represents any kind of culmination or vanguard of the science of management, or that it is optimal in any sense.

That it works very well is undeniable. US companies, managed in the American way, are to a significant extent the creators of the modern world. They dominate the international *Fortune* 500, and their brands are in demand everywhere. But this does not mean that other management models or styles will not emerge that are better, in some ways or in some circumstances, any more than the dominance of the US auto industry in the 1960s meant that the American way of making cars would never be challenged.

Nor does it mean the American management style is irredeemably set in its ways.

Knowing, doing, being

In the wake of revelations of management failings during the 2007–08 financial crisis, and pre-crisis scandals at Enron, WorldCom, and Tyco, Srikant Datar, David Garvin, and Patrick Cullen of HBS proposed a major reform of management education in their book

Rethinking the MBA: Business Education at a Crossroads.[3] They said that the *problématique* of management can be divided into three components: knowing, doing, and being.

Managers need to *know* the facts, frameworks, and theories that make up the "core understanding" of the management profession. Examples include the forces determining industry structure, the meaning and measurement of return on capital, and the "Four Ps" of marketing (product, price, place, promotion).

To *do*, managers need the skills, capabilities, and techniques that lie at the heart of the practice of effective management. Examples include executing tasks as a team member, implementing a project, conducting performance reviews, delivering a presentation, selling a product, and innovating.

The *being* component consists of values, attitudes, and beliefs that comprise the manager's world view and professional identity. These include behavior exemplifying integrity, honesty, and fairness, an awareness of his or her strengths and weaknesses, the treatment of others, and the purposes and goals of the organization.

The authors argue that without the *doing* skills, *knowing* is of little value, but that *doing* skills will be ineffective and lack direction without the self-awareness and reflections on values and beliefs that come from developing *being*. The weaknesses of western management training are that it tends to overemphasize and be insufficiently critical of the *knowing* (many theories and models are useful, but all are flawed, in one way or another), that it takes insufficient account of organizational realities in the *doing*, and neglects the *being*. These weaknesses make the MBA-trained professional manager less effective in a "real" world characterized by information overload, growing complexity, and an accelerating rate of change.

The emerging Chinese management model, sketched out in more detail in Chapter 7, places more emphasis on *being* and *doing,* and tends to develop its *knowing* on the run. One reason for this is that an important part of *knowing* in China is knowing what the government is planning to do, and how that may change the business environment. But as it happens, treating knowledge as provisional and applying what might be called "fuzzy logic," as opposed to the established, objective logic of the western tradition, could prove a good way to manage and process information overload.

If, as Datar, Garvin, and Cullen have suggested, western management education will place more emphasis in future on *being*, it could be said to be moving towards the management model that is emerging in the circumstances prevailing in modern China.

Time and place

Management models are the creatures of time and circumstances, and of the cultural, political, industrial, and economic environments in which they evolve. We should not expect, still less hope, that the emerging Chinese model of management will conform perfectly to the western style. It will be informed by, but not be derived from other styles. and its practitioners will not claim, as practitioners of the western model often claim, that their way of doing business is the best way everywhere, for everyone. No attempt will be made to export it, but it will be important even so, because of China's size and the influence its companies and managers will have in the world of business.

It is impossible to describe the Chinese management model, because it has yet to emerge as a distinctive model in its own right. But there are some clues about what it might be like, and how it might develop. It is likely, for instance, that it will retain elements of the western style, if only because the so-called "sea-turtles" educated at the western B-schools will maintain links between the two management cultures. It will also resemble the American model in the central role it assigns to entrepreneurs. But this will not be in emulation of the American model.

The entrepreneur has always played a key role in China. The entire socio-economic history of China can be seen as the endless ebb and flow of influence and power between "merchants" (entrepreneurs) on the one hand, and "administrators" (government) on the other. The merchants are the engine, the administrators are the governor. The engine has a hunger for wealth – the governor has a vision of what is good for the people. In the past, administrators were agents of emperors. Today they are agents of the Chinese Communist Party (CCP), representing the people of China. The balance between the two has been, and is still being, maintained by the acceptance by each of the necessity of the other, and a recognition on both sides of mutual dependence.

This is quite different from the relationship between business and government in the United States. There is no sense of partnership between the US government and US business. The latter accepts the necessity of the former, and the taxes it levies, because it values social and political stability, but it expects, and is for the most part given, freedom to do what it wants within the law. Governments in America and elsewhere in the West have policies with which they buy votes, but these do not amount to visions of the "good" for society. They have no direction comparable to the CCP's; no long-term intent.

This laissez-faire approach of western governments is reflected in an acceptance of the individual as the primary agent. Although, as noted above, merchants play a key role in China, their activities are restrained by administrators in the interests of the community as a whole. The idea of the non-owning "stakeholder," despite its current popularity in the West, is fundamentally incompatible with the western idea of the company as a mechanism for creating value for shareholders. It makes perfect sense—is almost a statement of the obvious—in China.

Another contrast between China and America that will create a very different style of management in China lies in the differences between the host cultures within which their management cultures evolved. The American culture, as opposed to the mainly European cultures that contributed to it, is barely three centuries old. China's culture has evolved over the millennia. Some trace the origins back to the Shang dynasty, thought to have come to power in 1600–1500 BC, and to have ruled for 500 years. A culture so ancient, and until quite recently so separate from, and untouched by, other cultures, is bound to be reflected in the Chinese management style, and to endow it with distinctively Chinese qualities, not evident in management styles that evolved elsewhere.

Culture, government, and entrepreneurs

China's culture contributes a spiritual component, the government provides the context and the environment —the land, as it were—and China's entrepreneurs and merchants have contributed the energy.

Box 3.1 Guo Zhenxi

Director of CCTV-2

Guo Zhenxi
Source: CCTV-2

Guo Zhenxi acknowledges that a television station is not a typical
business organization, but says that CCTV-2 (CCTV's business
channel) has a unique vantage point, because it has grown up
with Chinese private companies, and chronicled the development
of their business models and of the Chinese economy as a
whole.

In his view what attracts foreign observers and makes them keen to
listen to Chinese voices, and analyze the so-called Chinese model of
business, is the huge Chinese market and the growing success of
Chinese companies. A few years ago, it was hard for him to arrange
meeting with CEOs of international companies. These days, he meets
with multinational CEOs twice a week on average. But he says there
is still a huge gap between foreigners' understanding of China and the

facts. He identifies five qualities of the Chinese market that make it very different from markets elsewhere in the world:

- It is huge, which means enormous and diverse market needs.
- Consumption patterns are changing rapidly. Fifteen years ago, some goods were still in short supply. Now there is overcapacity in many industries, consumer bargaining power is increasing, and in some provinces, rural and urban economic disparities are narrowing.
- Chinese consumers trust advertisements. Unlike US television stations, the main television stations in China are state-owned. This makes them more trusted, and makes advertisements on these channels more credible.
- There is a strong impulse to conform among Chinese consumers, and under certain conditions, they are easy to influence. If you want to market in Chinese, it is crucial to create those conditions. Public media seem to be more effective for these purposes than specialty media.
- The Chinese market is a market of gifts. In western counties consumers buy products for themselves. In China, many goods, such as wine, and health and nutrition products, are bought for others.

Guo said that "every successful private company in China has a key leader in its management team. Co-operation within the management team is vital to the success of a company, but it's the key leader who calls the shots." This reflects Chinese history and culture. A key leader plays the role of the head of the family and his or her authority cannot be challenged. Guo says that Chinese companies are becoming increasingly standardized and systematic, but he believes the key leader will continue to play an important role.

Chinese companies and the management styles of the key leaders are evolving, according to Guo:

> Several years ago, the structures of Chinese companies were very simple. People didn't have the concept of company culture. In recent years, more and more companies are becoming standardized and systematic. But all the improvements are in response to local markets. The "sea

turtles" don't have as many advantages as they used to have when starting a business.

Guo says that after 30 years of high-speed development, it is high time to focus on the Chinese management model. "Management styles are closely related to cultures," he says. "This is especially true in oriental countries, such as China, Japan, and Korea. In the West management focuses more on the technical method."

He sees Chinese management as having evolved, by stages. The first stage was learning from the western model, which lasted 30 years. The second stage was Chinese entrepreneurs gradually finding their own way of managing, by adapting the western model to the Chinese environment. But Guo admits that different Chinese companies might have different ways of managing. "It's difficult to reach a simple conclusion on the Chinese management model," he says. "Some of them are organized, and others are random. Whatever model entrepreneurs choose, the only test will be effectiveness." Haidilao Hotpot (see page 69) retains traditional elements in its management style, for example, and there are no vice-presidents at Wahaha (see page 141): department heads report directly to the CEO. Most Chinese small and medium-sized enterprises (SMEs) are family-owned. Despite this variety, however, Guo believes that the western management thinking has provided a base for and made other valuable contributions to the establishment of the Chinese model.

Guo identifies key differences between the outcomes of the western and Chinese management styles. Relatively equal distributions of income are more acceptable in the Chinese organizations, and labor turnover rates in Chinese companies are generally lower than those in western-owned companies. He attributes the high turnover rates of Chinese employees in international companies to the difficulty Chinese employees experience in being accepted and feeling a sense of belonging in international companies, because of what seems to them an alien corporate culture.

As a media person himself, Guo believes the Chinese financial media accelerate the development of the Chinese business environment, by passing on the western management model, keeping

Chinese business people well informed, helping them to think about and develop the new management model, and reporting the successes and progress of Chinese entrepreneurs. He believes the Chinese financial media are more powerful and have a deeper influence on Chinese consumers and business people than their counterparts abroad.

Luyang Jiang and the author

Spirit, land, energy. These are the pillars on which a distinctively Chinese management style is being built, and from which it will draw inspiration. Each will be examined in more detail in the next three chapters.

It will be important to remember, however, that they interact with each other constantly, in unpredictable ways. The management style that emerges from this interaction cannot be predicted on the basis of an understanding of the influence of each pillar. The puzzle of the Chinese management style reflects the puzzle of China itself. Both are like a jigsaw puzzle in reverse. Although each piece may seem intelligible and relatively simple on its own, the whole that emerges from them is complicated, and sometimes counter-intuitive.

To get an idea of how the three pillars interact and often reflect each other, it is worth recalling how the American experiment began.

For Deng Xiaoping, usually seen as the leading architect of modern China, the bottom line—the ultimate objective—was the survival of the CCP as the governing institution in China. He, and other Chinese leaders after him, never took that survival for granted. In 1978, Deng believed the way to maintain the CCP's rule was for the party to feed the people first and then to give them a realistic expectation of a better life. His vision for achieving these objectives was to pursue the American Dream in the American way, because at that time the American way seemed the best way.

Deng had no plan comparable in its strategic grandeur to the Great Leap Forward to realize his vision, but he had faith in the people of China: in their ability to find ways to feed themselves, and to create a better life for themselves. They did not disappoint him. The decision not to prosecute the farmers of Xiaogang, but rather to legalize their illegal experiment and endorse it as a model for decollectivization, was scarcely the stuff of grand strategy, but it had consequences as beneficial as the Great Leap Forward's were disastrous.

Deng was equally sanguine about the spontaneous entrepreneurialism that transformed communally owned Township and Village Enterprises (TVEs) created during the Cultural Revolution into the seeds of an essentially capitalist economy. He had not expected it, but he saw it as a positive development, worthy of official endorsement, that could help realize his vision of a prosperous China, with a strong American-style economy.

Deng, and those who succeeded him as leaders, were like theatrical directors with misty visions of what they want, who are content to rely on lightly regulated experiments within the ensemble to fill in the detail. "To cross the river, you have to feel the stones." You cannot see the stones or locate them on a map, but if you take one step at a time, in what appears to be the right direction, you should make it across. It is the policy of a pragmatic opportunist: if an unexpected trend develops or event occurs, which seems to be consistent with the guiding vision, let it run.

This approach to the "modernization" of China is reflected in what may emerge as an important, and distinctively Chinese, contribution to the development of business management, discussed in Chapter 7.

Summary

- The American management model/style originated in the mid-nineteenth century.
- It is a creature more of accident and circumstance than of the inexorable working out of economic laws.
- American B-school academics advocate reforms of the MBA degree that, if implemented, would move western management education towards the emerging Chinese management model.
- A distinctively Chinese management model is emerging from the interplay of the "spirit, land, energy" trinity in modern China.
- It is emerging gradually, in much the same way as the modern Chinese economy emerged gradually from Deng Xiaoping's reforms.

Notes

1 Alfred Chandler (1977) *The Visible Hand: The Managerial Revolution in American Business,* Cambridge, Mass.: Harvard University Press.
2 John Kotter (1995) *The New Rules: How to Succeed in Today's Post-Corporate World*, New York: Free Press.
3 Srikant Datar, David Garvin, and Patrick Cullen (2010) *Rethinking the MBA: Business Education at a Crossroads,* Cambridge, Mass.: Harvard Business Press.

CHAPTER 4

Spirit

In January 2010 a battle was fought in Chinese cinemas, variously depicted as a confrontation between the forces of modernity on the one hand and conservatism on the other, between western liberalism and Chinese authoritarianism, between free trade and protectionism, and between high-tech froth and serious philosophical commentary.

The antagonists were *Avatar*, James Cameron's 3-D blockbuster, and *Confucius*, a locally produced biopic of China's famous philosopher and teacher. It was a one-sided confrontation. In the battle for urban moviegoers, *Confucius* was no match for *Avatar*'s expensive and dazzling display of state-of-the art cinematography, and *Avatar*'s Chinese distributors were no match for state-run China Film Group Corporation (CFGC), which decides how long and where foreign films can be shown.

When *Avatar* proved wildly popular in China, the CFGC restricted its screenings to 3-D cinemas, to give *Confucius* a chance. The Chinese blogosphere erupted, and parallels were drawn between *Avatar*'s plot —developers appropriating land and evicting the inhabitants—and the civil unrest following so-called land-grabs by local officials in Southern China. The CFGC later relented, and the restrictions on *Avatar* screenings were lifted.

Outsiders were left with the impression that Confucianism had been tested in a confrontation with modernism and been found wanting by Chinese people. Not at all. Confucianism is alive and thriving in China, and is an important part of the cultural environment within which the new Chinese management style is emerging.

A book of this kind can, of course, merely put a few scratches on the surface of China's rich and ancient culture, but a review of some of the ideas and principles that have infused the national psyche over the millennia will help us understand something of the cultural provenance of the new Chinese style of management.

The first thing to say is that there is much, much more to Chinese culture than Confucius. Confucianism is an important component of the Chinese culture, but for westerners and many Chinese it is also a label, or brand, representing an accumulation of folk wisdom that dates back long before Confucius, and in which Confucius and other Chinese thinkers and philosophers found their inspiration.

I Ching

If the stature of a cultural artefact is measured by the length of its reach across the ages, the *I Ching* (the Book of Changes) has no peer.

The origins of the *I Ching* divination system are too ancient to be established with certainty, but their principles are traditionally attributed to a probably mythical shaman, King Fu Xi (c. 2800 BC), to whom the eight "trigrams" were said to have been divulged supernaturally. By the time of the legendary shaman/engineer, Yu (circa 2100 BC), the trigrams had developed into the 64 hexagrams described in the book *Lian Shan* (continuous mountains). Fu Xi and Yu are also seen as early followers of Daoism (see below), with which the *I Ching* is intimately connected.

The language of the divination system is binary. "Yes" is a simple unbroken line (traditionally a yarrow stalk), and "No" is a broken line (two shorter yarrow stalks). These are combined in groups of three (trigrams), giving eight possible combinations, representing all that happens in heaven and on earth. The oracular focus is not on the trigrams themselves, but on the transformations of one into another: from son into father, for example, or water into air. The completion of the *I Ching* divination system still in use today was achieved by combining pairs of trigrams to produce 64 hexagrams.

Divination systems have been popular everywhere throughout history (the Tarot, the crystal ball, the oracle at Delphi, the witches in *Macbeth*). The popularity of the *I Ching* divination system in China today reflects the characteristic fatalism of the Chinese—"What will be, will be"—and a corresponding recognition of the role of luck, both of which will influence the emerging Chinese management model.

The western management model tries to minimize the role of luck in business (not always successfully, as the 2007–08 financial crisis showed), with detailed statistical analysis, probability theory, and arrays of risk management techniques. The Chinese management model is more tolerant of or more Daoist about (see below) the impact on a business of good and bad luck.

But the *I Ching*'s focus on movement and change endowed it with the potential to become more than a divination system. Fate was fixed in other divination systems. Nothing could be done to change it. *I Ching* predictions were provisional, because change was changeable. The Book of Changes became a book of wisdom and morality, when the question "What will be?" was followed by "What then should I do?"

The transformation was attributed to King Wen, founder of the Zhou dynasty (1045–221 BC) and his son, the duke of Zhou. They assigned to the hexagrams counsels for conduct. From being passive victims of an inexorable fate, individuals became, with the flow of change divined by the hexagrams, co-shapers of their destinies. The sooner they acted on what the yarrow stalks revealed, the better, because it is only in its early germinal stage that change is controllable.

This idea that individuals can control change to some extent if they can divine its nature early enough may also become part of the Chinese management style. It counsels managers to look for the embryonic, to be watchful and alert, to scan their environment constantly for faint signals heralding profound change.

Guo Zhenxi, the director of CCTV-2 , was expressing this idea when he cautioned against the indiscriminate use of western management tools. "Even with very good tools some western companies fail; you need to be connected to the environment and culture to apply these tools successfully; otherwise you will achieve the opposite of the intended results" (see page 58).

The underlying idea of the *I Ching* philosophy is change, but those who understand change shift their attention from the transitory to the immutable law ruling all change. This is the "Dao" of Lao Tzu (see below), derived from the "great primal beginning," the circle divided into light and dark, yang and yin. Change is the constant transformation of the one into the other: from success to failure, from advantage to disadvantage, from loss to profit. Nothing stays the same, except the way, the path, the Dao.

Confucianism

Confucianism is an obsolete relic of China's cultural past that is obstructing progress; an underlying essence of China, transcending the passage of the centuries; a collection of ideas, some of which are outmoded, but some of which are contributing to a new cultural synthesis. At different times the teachings of Confucius have been seen in China as all of these things.

During the Cultural Revolution (1966–71) those who spoke well of Confucius were branded counter-revolutionaries, and risked arrest and execution. A photograph of Chairman Mao adorned the cover of a newspaper announcing the desecration of Confucius's grave in Qufu.

Today, Confucianism is almost China's official religion. In recent years "Confucius Institutes," non-profit institutions that promote the Chinese language and Chinese culture, have been opened, by the Office of Chinese Language Council International (Hanban) based in Beijing, in universities throughout the world. By the end of 2009 there were almost 300, including 46 in the United States, 10 in the United Kingdom, 8 in Italy, 6 in Australia, 5 in Germany, and 3 in France.

It is "almost" China's religion, because although it has spiritual elements, Confucianism is not strictly speaking a religion. It is more a code of practice of how society should be "ordered" and how people should behave.

"Confucius" (551–479 BC) is the Roman name given by Jesuits in the seventeenth century to Kong Fuzi ("Master Kong"), an itinerant teacher who lived during the Eastern Zhou dynasty (771–221 BC), when China was a collection of small warring states. It was a creative as well as a turbulent period, to which the origins of Legalism and Daoism can also be traced back (see below). Disturbed by the violence of his times and what he saw as the lack of a moral compass, Confucius offered himself as a counselor to a number of rulers. As with Socrates, the only record of his teaching are the recollections of his disciples, recorded in the *Analects*.

Confucius was influenced profoundly by the *I Ching*, and is thought to have written *Shi Yi* (Ten Wings), a collection of commentaries on the Book of Changes. He is reported, in the *Analects*, to have said, when standing on a river bank: "Everything flows on and on like this river, without pause, day and night." This may appear to be at odds with Confucius's reputation as an advocate of stability and conformity. But rivers have banks—things change according to unchanging laws. There is change, and there is continuity.

Change is the religion in western management. Continuity is likely to be seen as equally important in the emerging Chinese management model.

Confucianism consists of a number of key ideas and principles that are necessary for the good ordering of society. The most important of these is *li* (ritual): not the formal, repetitive actions the word denotes in English, but acceptable, morally correct behavior through which people can exhibit their best qualities. Order—not just orderliness, also a well-ordered social structure—emerges from following ritual correctly. Order does not oppress. It allows moral and ethical behavior (*de*) to flourish. In an ordered, and morally correct society, there is no need for the use of force. The morally correct person aspires to become a *junzi* (a gentlemen or person of integrity).

Hierarchy is essential to maintain stability. Servants should obey their masters, subjects should obey their rulers, children should obey their parents, and wives should obey their husbands. From this hierarchical structure come the ideas of *ren* (benevolence), *yi* (propriety), *xiao* (filial piety), and *zhong* (loyalty). The idea of the family plays a central role in Confucian thought, from the basic level of parents and their children, through, by analogy, to the state and its people, and to the chief executive and his or her employees.

If a person in authority, whether a king, master, or parent, abused his power, he would be in violation of the norms of what was right and correct. This idea that the emperor is *in loco parentis* to his subjects and must never abuse his power predates Confucius. It is thought to have emerged during the Western Zhou dynasty (1045–771 BC), when questions were asked about the morality of the successful Zhou invasion of the Yellow River Valley and subsequent ousting of the Shang dynasty, which had ruled China for 500 years.

The Zhous' answer to their critics was the Mandate of Heaven (*tian*

Box 4.1 Zhang Yong

Chairman, Haidilao Hotpot Company

Zhang Yong with customers
Source: Luyang Jiang

We met Zhang Yong, the chairman and founder of the Haidilao Hotpot restaurant chain, on "mother's day" at the first Hotpot restaurant in Beijing. He goes there once a month. We asked if we could take a picture of him at a table by the window, with some customers. He seemed shy, but reluctantly agreed. When we introduced him to the customers—a married couple taking the husband's parents out to celebrate mother's day—the mother said it was the first time she and her husband had been there, but that her son and his wife were regulars. When we left them, Zhang said their lunch was on him.

Zhang sees himself as fortunate in having been born in 1970. Those of his generation grew up as Deng Xiaoping's opening-up policy was getting into its stride. He says it was "a golden age for learning and accepting knowledge." He read voraciously at technical school, and says he acquired a sense of his own worth from books, and the belief, which has inspired him to focus on employee welfare at his company, that people are born equal and should be treated equally.

He regards China's food and catering market as relatively open and competitive, but so large that most restaurants in China, unlike those in Europe and America, can make a profit without paying much attention to their customers' requirements. Zhang says the reason for the success of Haidilao Hotpot is that the company understands employees' and customers' requirements, and goes out of its way to meet them.

Haidilao has over 10,000 employees. Zhang sees himself and acts as their father. He says most are from the poor areas of China. "They are young adults driven by a strong wish to change their families' lives, by working hard. But they don't understand how to involve themselves in the life of big cities, like Beijing and Shanghai." Zhang encourages them to make friends with local people, and gives them the money to do so.

Most Hotpot sites are rented. Zhang says the company would be more profitable if it bought sites, but he prefers to invest in growth and the welfare of his employees. He says that he is more interested in developing his people than in acquiring fixed assets.

At present Zhang's authority cannot be challenged in Haidilao, but he is trying to decentralize decision-making. Take site selection. He was the only decision-maker a few years ago, but now the retail managers have the right to propose sites. For the rest, Zhang says people manage themselves. Ordinary waiters, for example, learn the right thing to do from feedback from their work performance.

He sees some cultural differences between West, and East, but says customers' requirements are similar everywhere, and as long as a company treats its employees and customers well, it should be able to succeed anywhere. He wants to expand into Europe at some stage. He acknowledges that Haidilao's existing management style may not be appropriate for western employees, because of their different educational and cultural backgrounds, but believes his company can learn to adapt to the European environment.

He does not think the Chinese management model goes much beyond the western management model. The key point, as he sees it, is how far you go in adopting the western model. For instance, labor unions are very powerful in western countries, but they are not in China. If a western company goes too far in recognizing unions, that might not be proper in China.

Venture capital funds (VCs) have recently expressed an interest in investing in Haidilao, and bringing it to market. Zhang has so far rejected such overtures. "The main priorities for Haidilao now are developing standard processes for its operations and logistics, and training employees," he says. "Haidilao will become listed once it is fully prepared."

Luyang Jiang and the author

ming); the idea that rulers receive a mandate from heaven that is conditional on their good behavior. If they misbehave, they can be deposed. This idea that power is conditional on the good behavior of those who wield it is deeply embedded in the attitudes of the Chinese to their rulers, whether emperors, presidents, chairmen, or paramount leaders. It is also evident in the way power is wielded in Chinese companies. Zong Qinghou, chairman and CEO of Wahaha, China's most successful soft drinks group, says that "employees … have the right to judge their boss's performance" (see page 141). As Guo Zhenxi put it, "every successful private company in China has a 'key leader' in its management team, who plays the role of the head of the family, and his or her authority can't be challenged" (see page 58).

The idea of the group, whether family, organization, or the people at large, as the unit of agency in the Confucian world view left no room for "ego-tripping" and self-advancement. Individualism and putting oneself forward is selfish and petty, and nor did Confucian thought respect the urge to make money or seek profit. This aspect of Confucianism was evident in the way Chinese companies handled the fallout from the 2007–08 financial crisis. Instead of cutting staff numbers, as is customary in the West in difficult times, the common response was across-the-board salary reductions.

Long after Confucius's death, when China had been unified into one state, further developments of Confucian thought gave the emperor a role in the ordering of society. He was the mediator between, and the bridge connecting, the spiritual and earthly worlds, and thus a key element in the hierarchy that underpinned the Chinese empire.

Although not influential in his own lifetime, Confucius cast a long shadow over Chinese history. His teachings, as passed down in the *Analects*, came to be seen by rulers from the Han dynasty (220 BC–221 AD) onwards as an exemplary creed for the people, because they provided an ethical as well as a rational justification for strong and stable government.

Legalism

But Confucianism had some problems for rulers. Its proscription of force and violence, and its emphasis on mutual obligations between superiors and inferiors, did not always sit well with the exigencies of *realpolitik* in ancient China. A more attractive philosophy for rulers in this respect was Legalism, or the School of Law advocated by Han Feizi (281–233 BC).

Legalism was an altogether darker philosophy than Confucianism. It assumed people are motivated by fear and greed, and will act badly, unless restrained by strict laws and harsh punishments. It focuses on the ruler, who controls the state with his power (*shi*), certain techniques (*shu*), and laws (*fa*). It had an obvious appeal to rulers during the Warring States period (463–222 BC), and was adopted with enthusiasm by the Qin king, Zheng. A rigid hierarchy of status and a tight legal framework were established. The Qin dynasty became so strong as a consequence that by 221 BC, it had conquered all of the northern states and for the first time China was united under one ruler.

Zheng changed his name to Shi Huangdi (First Emperor) and extended the writ of Legalism throughout his realm. China was divided into districts, governed by local officials. Weights and measures were standardized, and writing was standardized and updated, establishing the characters still used today.

But the yoke of Legalism proved too harsh particularly when, in an effort to suppress dissent, the emperor burned all books outside his own library, apart from those dealing with practical subjects, such as agriculture and medicine. This act of vandalism earned Shi Huangdi the lasting hatred of Confucian scholars. The ancient text of the *I Ching*, hidden away by peasants, was a notable survivor of the book-burning.

Soon after Shi Huangdi died in 210 BC, escorted to his grave by an army of 7,000 life-sized terracotta warriors, the Qin empire began to break up. The third and last Qin emperor was defeated in 206 BC by a former bandit chief, Liu Bang, who declared himself the emperor Gao Zu. So began the Han dynasty, which was to rule China for four centuries.

But Legalism was not buried with Shi Huangdi. Its attractions, for emperors, ensured its survival, in a partnership with Confucianism known as *ru wai, nei fa*: being outwardly Confucian, but inwardly Legalistic. A thousand years before Bismarck advocated his "iron fist in a velvet glove," Confucian morals were promoted for public consumption, to discourage challenges and reduce unrest, while the law was reserved as a tool of authoritarian control, should a need arise. The partnership between the two fundamentally incompatible philosophies of Legalism on the one hand, and Confucianism on the other remains an important theme in China's political culture to this day. Mao Zedong favored Legalism. Although Confucianism has since become the official philosophy, the iron fist of Legalism is still held in reserve for those occasions when the border dividing acceptable from unacceptable behavior is crossed.

Daoism

When developing his doctrine of Legalism Han Feizi was influenced by the Daoist book, the *Dao De Jing* (The Book of the Way).

Daoism is thought to have emerged from a shamanic tradition dating back to the Ice Age. The structure of the universe was divulged to the shaman, King Fu Xi (see above), in the form of a framework for thought. Several centuries later another shaman, Yu, designed an irrigation system that protected his country from flooding, and divined the nature of the universe Fu Xi had described: continuous flux. The combination of structure and nature produced the *I Ching* (see above).

During the Warring States period (463–222 BC) the kings sought the advice of itinerant sages, among whom was Lao Tzu, supposed author of the *Dao de Jing*. The book preached a return to shamanic values and living in accordance with the rhythms of nature.

Lao Tzu's Daoist sage was an active member of society, who applied Daoist principles to every aspect of life, including politics, in his efforts to restore peace and harmony to the world. Chuang Tzu, a contemporary of Lao Tzu, taught a more passive Daoism. A Daoist sage should having nothing to do with affairs of state, but should instead seek spiritual integrity by withdrawing from a corrupt and fragmented everyday world.

Because, in Daoism, the idea of heresy is a heresy, Daoist thought has spawned numerous sects, of which the most popular is philosophical Daoism, with its idea of achieving an internal balance through practices and disciplines such as *Tai Chi*.

Lao Tzu was deeply influenced by the *I Ching*, and particularly its idea of constant change within unchanging laws. Daoists see strife and dissent as a consequence of constant striving which brings us up against obstacles and opposition. People should cease to strive and go with the flow, the way, the path (*Dao*).

In the West, Daoism has been seen as a prescription for meditation and the search for serenity, with no political connotations of any kind. That was not how the Legalist Han Feizi (see above) saw it. He interpreted the *Dao De Jing* as a political treatise, which assumed ordinary people were subject to natural laws they were obliged to obey. Rulers promulgated the *Dao*, which played a role in the lives of ordinary people much like the weather. Resistance was futile if not impossible. All that ordinary people could do was "go with the flow," like driftwood in a river. Han Feizi advised rulers to get on with ruling, leave the people in ignorance of affairs of state, and treat them like "straw dogs"; a reference to a passage in the *Dao de Jing*: "Heaven and Earth are not human. They regard all things as straw dogs."

Although China's rulers today are Confucian rather than Daoist and see themselves as parents of the people, rather than as masters of straw dogs, there is a hint of Daoism in the way the CCP's policies and decisions are perceived. To most Chinese people, they are like the weather; they can be adapted to, and often exploited (as when, for instance, a property developer makes a killing, by buying land after a change in social housing policy is heralded in a speech at the National People's Congress), but they cannot be resisted. Going with the flow is the only option.

Daoism prescribes acceptance of what happens, but also persistence in the face of setbacks, and an admirable stoicism. The story is told of an emperor standing on his palace wall watching the market below. He sees a merchant walking through the stalls carrying some porcelain plates. Someone bumps into him, he drops the plates, and they shatter on the ground. The merchant leaves the broken plates where they are, turns round and begins walking back the way he had come. The emperor sends a servant to bring the merchant to him and asks the merchant why he has left his broken plates. The merchant explains that the market will remain open for some time yet and he is going to get some more plates.

If you encounter difficulties, press on. Go with the flow.

Stories such as these, often featuring an enlightened emperor and a peasant or merchant, play an important role in the education and training of senior CCP officials (see Chapter 5).

Sun Tzu

Some historians still question whether Sun Tzu, putative author of one of the world's most famous military texts, *The Art of War*, is an authentic historical figure. Tradition has it, however, that Sun Tzu was a successful general at the end of the Spring and Autumn Period of the Eastern Zhou dynasty (770–464 BC), and wrote *The Art of War* in the Warring States period (464–222 BC).

The book comprises 13 short essays on the philosophy of war. It is an attempt, widely regarded as successful, to apply Daoist thought to military matters. It soon became the basis of orthodox military theory in China, and required reading for those preparing for exams for imperial appointments to military positions.

Sun Tzu's ideal military commander is an enlightened Daoist. It is this spiritual dimension that distinguishes his book most clearly from other well-known military texts, such as the German Carl von

Clausewitz's *On War*. Its scope was also much wider. In addition to introducing military concepts, such as terrain classification, the book dealt with public administration and planning, diplomacy, and foreign policy. Sun Tzu saw the cultivation of good relationships with other nations as essential to the health of a state.

Although the language seems strange to western ears—generals must be "serene and inscrutable," and able to comprehend "unfathomable plans"—no other Chinese book has been more widely read and heeded beyond China's borders.

The Art of War reached Japan in the first century AD, and adoption of its principles was in evidence during the unification of Japan. Mastery of Sun Tzu's teaching became an integral part of a samurai's education. A summary translation of the book by the French Jesuit Father Amiot became available in Europe towards the end of the eighteenth century. Napoleon Bonaparte admired it, and followed its teachings during his initially successful attempts to unify Europe. Admiral Togo Heihachiro, who led Japan to victory in the Russo–Japanese War, was an avid reader, and Mao Zedong attributed his 1949 victory over Chiang Kai-shek and the Kuomintang partly to *The Art of War*.

Sun Tzu's teachings were brought to the attention of the American military by their defeat in Vietnam by General Vo Nguyen Giap, for whom *The Art of War* was said to be a bible. The US secretary of state, Henry Kissinger, was an early American convert, and the book is on the Marine Corps Professional Reading Program. Generals Norman Schwarzkopf and Colin Powell are said to have followed Sun Tzu's principles of deception, speed, and attacking weakness during the first Gulf War in the 1990s.

The Art of War has been consumed in the West in the form of aphorisms and extracts, some of the most celebrated of which are:

> All warfare is based on deception.

> Let your plans be dark and as impenetrable as night, and when you move, fall like a thunderbolt.

> If your enemy is secure at all points, be prepared for him. If he is in superior strength, evade him. If he is temperamental,

seek to irritate him. Pretend to be weak, that he may grow arrogant. If he is taking his ease, give him no rest. If his forces are united, separate them. If sovereign and subject are in accord, put division between them. Attack him where he is unprepared. Appear where you are not expected.

Keep your friends close, and your enemies closer.

If you know your enemies and know yourself, you will not be imperiled in a hundred battles.

Be extremely subtle, even to the point of formlessness. Be extremely mysterious, even to the point of soundlessness.

The supreme art of war is to subdue the enemy without fighting.

In the practical art of war, the best thing of all is to take the enemy's country whole and intact.

Victorious warriors win first and then go to war.

Speed is the essence of war. Take advantage of the enemy's unpreparedness; travel by unexpected routes and strike him where he has taken no precautions.

A leader leads by example, not by force.

Opportunities multiply as they are seized.

He who knows when he can fight and when he cannot, will be victorious.

If words of command are not clear and distinct, if orders are not thoroughly understood, the general is to blame. But if his orders are clear, and the soldiers nevertheless disobey, then it is the fault of their officers.

Stories have also been passed down, to illustrate Sun Tzu's ideas and principles. One such, which illustrates the last of the above aphorisms, is that Sun Tzu's patron, king Helü of Wu, told him to demonstrate his skills as a commander by training a harem of 180 concubines to become soldiers. Sun Tzu divided the concubines into two companies, and appointed the king's two favorites as company commanders. He ordered the concubines to face right. They giggled. Sun Tzu turned to the king and explained that he, as the general, was responsible for ensuring that soldiers understood the commands given to them. He repeated the command, and again the concubines giggled. Sun Tzu ordered the execution of the commander concubines and told the king that, if the soldiers understood their general's commands and still did not obey, it was the fault of the officers, and that once a general was appointed it was the officers' duty to carry out the general's mission.

Western interest in *The Art of War* is not confined to the military establishment. Its ideas and principles have also been applied to sports, diplomacy, and personal lives. The book and its author crop up frequently in western business and management literature, too. Dick Fuld, former chief executive officer (CEO) of Lehman Bothers, the most conspicuous casualty of the 2007–08 financial crisis, is said to have referred to the failed investment bank's competitors as "enemies" whose throats must be "ripped out," and to have urged his employees to act as though they were "at war."

Whether Fuld had read *The Art of War* is not known, but it is likely that, although they would not use such intemperate language, many other US business leaders share Fuld's view of "business as war." Why else should Sun Tzu's principles have attracted such interest among western business writers?

Another interesting question is whether the emerging Chinese style of management will be as wedded to the idea of "business as war," and draw as much inspiration from Sun's teachings, as its American counterpart. Some Chinese entrepreneurs, such as Zhou Hongyi, the founder and CEO of search engine company Qihoo.com, certainly do (see page 159). Others prefer to see business as a game of Go, in which there is friendship between players who play a good game, and an ethos of cooperation and peaceful coexistence.

Enter the administrators

During the Han dynasty (206 BC–220 AD) the harsh Legalism of the Qin was replaced by a return to Confucianism. Gao Zu, the first of a long line of Han emperors, was a pragmatist, however, and saw no reason to dispense with all of the Qin legacy. He was content with the standardization of the language, and weights and measures, and a centralized system of power. But he was from peasant stock, and he and his successors dismantled the feudal system of aristocratic rule. They replaced it with a system run by officials and administrators appointed on merit.

This crucial shift from aristocratic to meritocratic rule in China was further developed by the sixth Han emperor, Wu Di, who acceded to the throne in 141 BC. He streamlined central government with an office of palace clerks, to issue edicts to the arms of government and screen the inflow of documents to the palace. Another significant innovation during Wu Di's rule was the establishment of a national university to train officials, entry to which was by a competitive examination.

This new, high-status administrative class remains a vital part of China's system of government to this day. The economic development of China can be seen, in one way, as a history of the relationship between China's administrators and merchants. The latter also had cause to be grateful to Wu Di. When not creating the world's first professional civil service he was expanding the empire by annexing several western and south-western states, and opening up the "Silk Road" trade route, along which Chinese merchants carried silk, tea, and spices across central Asia to Rome.

Religion

The Silk Road also carried some traffic of a less material kind in the other direction. The first spiritual import was Buddhism, said to have been brought to China by two monks, Kasyapa and Dharmaraksha, in 68 AD, at the invitation of the Emperor Ming (58 AD–75 AD), who had dreamed of a golden man with a shining halo, and was told such a being was known in the regions to the West.

Northern China proved fertile ground for Buddhism, which resembled in some respects both Confucianism and Daoism, to which Buddhism became very close as it adapted to local conditions. But towards the end of the Tang dynasty (618–907 AD) its foreign origins, the power of its monasteries and temples, and its injunctions to the devout to withdraw from society, in a culture that set much store by family life, led to its repression. Han Yu (768–824 AD), now widely regarded as among China's finest writers, wrote:

> Buddha was a man of the barbarians who did not speak the language of China …. His sayings did not concern the ways

of our ancient kings, nor did his manner of dress conform to their laws. He understood neither the duties that bind sovereign and subject, nor the affections of father and son.

In 845 AD Emperor Wu Zong ordered the destruction of 4,600 monasteries and 40,000 temples, and obliged 250,000 Buddhist monks and nuns to give up their monastic lives.

Buddhism revived during the Song dynasty (960–1278 AD) in partnership with Daoism and Confucianism under the ecumenical banner of "Three Religions Combining into One."

The religious cleansing of 845 had also expelled Christianity from China, introduced two centuries earlier, in its Nestorian form, by the Persian missionary Alopen. It did not return until the Mongol hegemony under the Khans and their Yuan successors. Nestorianism was reintroduced, and in 1294, contacts were established with the papacy through Franciscan missionaries.

But Christianity's roots in China were never as deep as Buddhism's, and Christians were expelled again during the Ming dynasty (1368–1644), during which China progressively severed its contacts with the outside world.

Towards the end the Ming dynasty the Italian mathematician Matteo Ricci and other Jesuits were welcomed at the imperial court, but Christianity's revival stalled again after the pope proscribed the Jesuits' policy of adapting their religion to traditional Chinese practices. Christianity began to make more headway during the Qing dynasty (1644–1911). New waves of missionaries introduced Russian Orthodoxy in the early eighteenth century, and Protestantism in the early nineteenth century. Missionary activity increased sharply after the First Opium War in 1842. Some leaders of the Chinese Republic, including Sun Yat-sen, were converts to Christianity.

Islam is said to have been brought to China in 651, 18 years after Muhammad's death and 16 years after the arrival of Christianity, but its influence on China as been more through the immigration of Muslims than through missionary work and evangelism.

Muslim merchants settled in Chinese cities during the Tang dynasty, and by the time of the Song dynasty had come to play a major role in Silk Road and sea-borne commerce. In 1070, the emperor Shenzong invited 5,300 Muslim men from Bukhara to settle in China to create a buffer zone between China and the Liao empire in the north-east. During the Yuan dynasty (1271–1368) Mongol emperors recruited many thousands of Persian, Arab, and Uyghur immigrants as administrators for their expanding empire.

Ming emperors also appointed Muslims to high offices of state. The first emperor, Zhu Yuanzhang, counted six Muslims among his most trusted generals, including Lan Yu, who led the imperial army to a decisive victory over the Mongols in 1388. Zheng He, an explorer and perhaps the most famous Chinese Muslim, led seven expeditions to the Indian Ocean, from 1405 to 1433. When Ming emperors became more introverted and China accordingly became more isolated, new immigration from Muslim countries was restricted. Earlier Muslim immigrants, now detached from their roots, went native. They spoke Chinese dialects, adopted Chinese names, and immersed themselves in the Chinese culture. Visible evidence of this cultural osmosis was provided by the gradual adoption of traditional Chinese shapes and styles in mosque architecture.

Statistics on the prevalence of religious belief or the lack of it are notoriously unreliable, but according to Philip Zuckerman, 59 percent (700 million) of the Chinese population are irreligious, and 8–14 percent (100–180 million) are atheist.[1] A survey by Shanghai University found that 31 percent of Chinese people over the age of 16 (300 million) considered themselves religious. About 200 million are Buddhists or Daoists or worship legendary figures, such as the Dragon King and the God of Fortune, and 40 million (12 percent of believers) are Christians.[2]

A particular difficulty with these statistics in China is whether or not several important belief systems are "religions." There is a strong spiritual dimension to Confucianism, for instance, in its ritual activities, and the inward search for the source of a moral order. But, unlike the so-called "religions of the book" (Judaism, Islam, and Christianity) there is no god at the centre of Daoism or Confucianism. There is a heaven or higher place, but no supreme being; no ultimate moral authority.

Buddhism, Christianity, and Islamism have made contributions to Chinese culture, but they have not changed it significantly. China has been and remains a secular, largely godless country, which has sought and found its moral compass in introspection, contemplation, and Confucian ritual (*li*), rather than in worship.

Maoism

The closest China came to monotheism was the personality cult that surrounded Mao Zedong. Most Westerners assume that Mao's twin disasters of the Great Leap Forward and the Cultural Revolution must surely have discredited the CCP leader in the eyes of Chinese people. Not at all. Most Chinese people agree with Deng Xiaoping's judgment that Mao was "70 percent good, 30 percent bad." As is the way with the selective memory of the Chinese, they focus on the "70 percent good."

Mao's two disastrous social experiments exposed the danger of what Deng called "ultra-leftism" in a country of over a billion people, but Mao as a revolutionary, rather than an administrator, is still revered as one of the architects of modern China. A picture of a relatively young Mao, during his revolutionary hero period, adorns Chinese bank notes.

Ye Maozhong, the founder and CEO of one of China's most successful marketing companies, Ye Maozhong Marketing, is not alone among the new generation of entrepreneurs in admiring Mao enormously. Ye devotes considerable amounts of time to the study of Mao's writing, and says he has "carried out Mao's thoughts without thinking" (see page 17).

As is the case with Sun Tzu's wisdom, Mao's wisdom is passed down through quotations and aphorisms, such as:

> An army without culture is a dull-witted army, and a dull-witted army cannot defeat the enemy.

> I have witnessed the tremendous energy of the masses. On this foundation it is possible to accomplish any task whatsoever.

> Let the people speak up. If they have good arguments, we listen to them; if they don't, we refute them.

> The only way to settle questions of an ideological nature or controversial issues among the people is by the democratic method, the method of discussion, of criticism, of persuasion

and education, and not by the method of coercion or repression.

Ask your subordinates about matters you don't understand or don't know, and do not lightly express your approval or disapproval.

Even if we achieve gigantic successes in our work, there is no reason whatsoever to feel conceited and arrogant. Modesty helps one to go forward, whereas conceit makes one lag behind.

Complacency is the enemy of study. We cannot really learn anything until we rid ourselves of complacency. Our attitude towards ourselves should be to be insatiable in learning and towards others to be tireless in teaching.

We shall support whatever our enemies oppose and oppose whatever our enemies support.

It is necessary to investigate both the facts and the history of a problem in order to study and understand it.

Despise the enemy strategically, but take him seriously tactically.

Kindness in words creates confidence. Kindness in thinking creates profoundness. Kindness in giving creates love.

In time of difficulties, we must not lose sight of our achievements.

If you want to know the taste of a pear, you must change the pear by eating it yourself.

In waking a tiger, use a long stick.

Our duty is to hold ourselves responsible to the people. Every word, every act and every policy must conform to the people's interests, and if mistakes occur, they must be corrected—that is what being responsible to the people means.

The last could have come from an ancient Chinese emperor. Although he turned in the end against all culture, Mao stood in imperial shoes when he acknowledged the Confucian responsibility of a ruler to the ruled.

Science and technology

In his book *Novum Organum,* published in 1620, English philosopher Francis Bacon wrote:

> Printing, gunpowder and the compass: These three have changed the whole face and state of things throughout the world; the first in literature, the second in warfare, the third in navigation; whence have followed innumerable changes, in so much that no empire, no sect, no star seems to have exerted greater power and influence in human affairs than these mechanical discoveries.

All three first emerged in China. Printing was invented during the Tang dynasty (618–907 AD), although printed cloth patterns dating back to before 220 AD survive. The magnetic attraction of a needle is mentioned in the *Louen-heng,* composed between 20 and 100 AD, although the first mentions of magnetized needles in Chinese literature did not appear until 1086.

Ge Hong, an alchemist living in the Three Kingdoms period (220–618 AD), recorded the chemical reaction when saltpetre, pine resin, and charcoal were mixed and heated. Another account suggests gunpowder was an incidental invention during the search by Daoist alchemists for the elixir of life. The world-shaping substance reached Arabia in the thirteenth century and Europe soon afterwards.

Other early Chinese inventions include the abacus, flying machines such as the kite and the Kongming lantern (a precursor of the hot air balloon), the shadow clock (a precursor of the sundial), the crossbow, the differential gear, the seismograph, the rocket, land and naval mines, and banknotes and minted coins.

In his book *Dream Pool Essays* (1088 AD), Shen Kuo wrote of dry docks for repairing ships, the navigational magnetic compass, the notion of true north, a geological theory of land formation, and climate change over enormous periods of time. He believed land was shaped by erosion, uplift, and silt depositions, and cited as evidence the horizontal strata of fossils in cliffs.

Shen also explained lunar and solar eclipses, and building on the conjecture of Sun Sikong (1015–1076) that rainbows were caused by interaction between sunlight and moisture in the air, proposed the phenomenon of atmospheric refraction.

The search for knowledge about the world and about the cosmos, and the development of new technology, were encouraged and sponsored by the emperors of a succession of Chinese dynasties, until the final Qing dynasty.

Scholars are still debating the question of why China's pioneering inventions and intellectual break-throughs failed to coalesce into "science," as the West understands the term, or invoke the Chinese equivalent of Europe's Industrial Revolution. Some suggest that it may have been the scorn heaped by Daoists on what seemed to them to be the absurdly presumptuous notion that human minds could ever grasp the divine complexity of the universe. Others offer a more prosaic explanation; that the Chinese population was large enough, labor was cheap enough, and agrarian productivity was high enough to render mechanization superfluous. Still others suggest that the *Hai Jin* (sea ban) prohibition of maritime activities imposed by the Qing dynasty in 1647, and the hatred of things European caused by the Opium Wars in the mid-nineteenth century (see Chapter 9), isolated China from rapid scientific and technological advance elsewhere at critical times. Political instability during the rule of the Qing empress, Cixi, the Republican war (1911–33), the Sino-Japanese war (1933–45), the Communist/Nationalist war (1945–49), and finally the Cultural Revolution, are also said to have isolated China from the global flows of scientific and technological knowledge.

When Deng Xiaoping became China's paramount leader, and identified science and technology as one of the "Four Modernizations" in his 1978 reforms, Chinese people began to rediscover their scientific curiosity, their appetite for the new, and the innate inventiveness that had enriched their culture for millennia.

Culture and management

China can no longer insulate itself from western culture as it has done in the past, and particularly not from the western business culture, from which Chinese entrepreneurs have learned much that is valuable, and with which they will remain on intimate terms in the global marketplace.

The objective of this chapter has been, not to show how these bits and pieces of China's cultural heritage are assembling themselves into a coherent Chinese management style that will owe nothing to other cultures, but to give some idea of the diversity, complexity, and richness of China's culture, and provide a few clues and tools for thought about what it might mean for Chinese management.

These clues include:

- Tension in China between the attractions of modernity and the call of a rich and ancient culture.
- Fatalism ("What will be, will be"), a corresponding recognition of the role of luck, and yet a belief that if change is spotted early enough, it can be controlled. Hence the need for constant scanning of the environment for weak signals heralding major change.
- Everything is changing all the time, but within unchanging natural laws. There is change and continuity.
- A well-ordered society emerges from morally correct behavior.
- Hierarchy is needed to maintain stability, but the power of rulers is conditional on their good behavior (the Mandate of Heaven).
- The group (family, organization, the people at large), rather than the individual, is the primary unit of agency. "Ego-tripping" and self-advancement are frowned upon.
- The combination of Confucianism and Legalism produced a policy for ruling equivalent to Bismarck's "iron fist in a velvet glove."
- Rulers promulgate the Dao, which then plays a role in the lives of ordinary people much like the weather.
- A decentralized system of government run by officials appointed on merit. China's economic development can be seen as a history of the relationship between administrators and merchants.
- China is officially atheist, and inherently secular. Fewer than one in three people are religious, and most of those are Buddhists and Daoists. Although there is no divine moral authority, the culture is saturated with transcendence and spirituality.
- The Chinese have a selective memory. Despite their experiences in the Great Leap Forward and the Cultural Revolution they still revere Mao Zedong as one of the architects of modern China.
- Science and technology have played in the past, and will play in the future, a vital role in the development of China's culture.

Readers who find it easy to divine the inferences they should draw about the emerging Chinese management style from these scratches on the surface of Chinese culture should read this chapter again. Confusion about the likely impact of the cultural legacy that will help to shape Chinese management is entirely appropriate.

Notes

1 Philip Zuckerman (2005) 'Atheism: contemporary rates and patterns', in *The Cambridge Companion to Atheism*, ed. Michael Martin, Cambridge: Cambridge University Press.
2 Untitled survey carried out by professors Tong Shijun and Liu Zhongyu, East China Normal University, Shanghai, 2007.

CHAPTER 5

Land

If one date has to be chosen for the birth of modern China and its system of government, May 4, 1919 will do as well as any.

Many of the building blocks had already been formed. As we saw in the previous chapter, the federal model of central direction and local execution had been established long ago, in the imperial era. The origin of the compact between ruler and ruled was also ancient and well-established. So too was the principle of administration by a well-trained, professional civil service at both central and local levels. The basic shape of China's economic and industrial policy, namely merchants lightly regulated and taxed by administrators, is also long-established.

What was lacking before 1919 was the idea of China.

A sense of nationhood finally emerged after what is still known as "the century of humiliation," beginning with defeat by the British in the Opium Wars of 1839–42 and 1856–60 (see Chapter 9), and the subsequent Treaties of Nanking and Tianjin, known as the "Unequal Treaties," in which Hong Kong was ceded to the British and "treaty ports," including Shanghai, were opened to unrestricted trade. In 1844, the United States and France concluded similar treaties with China. The humiliation many Chinese felt at these capitulations to "foreign devils" (*gwailo*) was partly responsible for the Taiping (1850–64), and Boxer (1899–1901) rebellions. These uprisings, defeat at sea in 1895 by Japan, and the Qing emperor's inability to prevent the Russians and Japanese fighting over Manchuria in 1904, led to the downfall of the Qing dynasty in 1911 and the ending of 3,000 years of dynastic rule in China.

When Yuan Shikai, the Republic of China's first president, died in

1916 after failing to restore Confucian rule, China split up into several regions with warlords fighting for dominance. The catalyst for the unification of China, and the emergence of the two parties (Nationalists and Communists, CCP) that would struggle for power during China's republican period (1912–49), was the treaty signed at the Paris Peace Conference after the First World War. It emerged later that Japan had negotiated a secret deal with Britain and France in 1917, which guaranteed that, if the Allies won, German colonies in China would be transferred to Japan. The Treaty of Versailles so stipulated.

The Chinese were outraged. Hundreds of Chinese students surrounded the hotel in Paris where China's delegates to the peace conference were staying, to prevent them from going to Versailles to sign. On May 4, 3,000 students gathered in front of Tian'anmen Gate leading into the Forbidden City in Beijing, and marched through the city demonstrating against the sell-out in Versailles. They broke into the house of the Republic of China's communications minister, Cao Rulin, assaulted his guests, destroyed his furniture, and set fire to his home. Order was restored when the police arrested 32 protestors, but the *I Ching* yarrow stalks had spoken. Great change had germinated.

The intense debates that followed the events of May 4 crystallized into the "May Fourth Movement," from which emerged the Nationalist and Communist parties. Both were passionately nationalist and they cooperated for a while, until China had rid itself of its foreign oppressor, Japan. The ensuing struggle between the two parties was settled in 1948 with the victory of the CCP.

Although the Nationalists were exiled to Taiwan, "nationalism" and interest in, and involvement with, world affairs became an integral part of government. Although much in China's system of government remained the same as in imperial times, and remains so to this day, with the CCP playing the role of emperor, this was new. The lesson of "the century of humiliation" had been learned. China had found itself as a nation, with borders to protect and vital interests to promote.

The sense of nationhood and the patriotism it engendered remain an important part of the Chinese social context within which foreign businesses operate in China. They are more likely to prosper if it is clear to local businesses and administrators what they can do, and what they know will help to strengthen China.

Two other lessons about government were learned in the first three decades of CCP rule. The first is that modern communications endow a central government that has a sense of direction—an ideology it wants to promote or an economic, or social vision it wants to realize—with enormous powers of persuasion and control. The Great Leap Forward and the Cultural Revolution would not have turned out so badly if they had not been promoted and implemented so skillfully.

The second important lesson learned during Mao Zedong's leadership is that, in a country of over a billion people, the consequences of policy mistakes or the misuse of the power to persuade and control can be horrific.

Since Mao's death China's leaders seem to have been more conscious of their ancient responsibilities to the people, under the Mandate of Heaven. They still use the power to persuade and control with great skill, but appear to be acutely aware of its limitations; of the dangers of pushing the enormous mass of China's population too hard or too fast in any direction. Decision-making is a protracted and painstaking process. Proposals are systematically "leaked" in the state-owned media well in advance, to allow their merits to be fully debated before they become policies. There are no sudden or radical changes in direction. It is more a matter of nudging trends and changing the emphasis or the priorities.

The Chinese government is seen by outsiders as authoritarian, and it is certainly true that Bismarck's iron fist makes an occasional appearance. For the most part, however, the authority wielded is the authority exercised by a father over his children, rather than the authority exercised by the strong over the weak.

The powers that be

The Communist Party is not the only political party in China. There are also eight officially recognized "democratic" parties:

- Chinese Nationalist Party
- China Democratic League
- China Democratic National Construction Association
- China Association for Promoting Democracy
- Chinese Peasants' and Workers' Democratic Party

- China Zhi Gong Dang
- Third September Society
- Taiwan Democratic Self-Government League.

They are all tiny compared with the CCP, and their members know that to attempt to become anything more would be suicidal, for the time being at any rate. Their existence is still significant, however, because it could facilitate any move in future from one party to multi-party democracy.

The CCP is the world's largest political party, with 70 million or more members. In addition to its lack of effective opposition, it differs from western-style political parties in a number of ways. It is involved in all areas of life, it has representatives at all levels of local government, in urban areas senior management posts at state-owned enterprises (SOEs) are in its gift, key government posts are only open to party members, and perhaps most striking of all to westerners, it is difficult to become a member. Applicants must be sponsored by existing members, are thoroughly vetted, and once admitted, must spend a year on probation being trained before becoming full members.

Perhaps the most significant change in the CCP's membership policy in recent years was the decision in 2002 to allow private business people (as opposed to SOE executives) to join. Some older members were strongly opposed to this blurring of the boundaries that have traditionally separated "merchants" from "administrators," but the move has led to a substantial influx of people with private-sector business experience.

The most important event in the CCP calendar is the National Party Congress (not to be confused with the National People's Congress). It is held once every five years, and has two important functions; to decide the policy vision for the next five years and to appoint members of the party's Central Committee, which appoints the 25-member (currently) Politburo, from which is chosen the nine-member (currently—it is always an odd number to prevent ties) Politburo Standing Committee (PSC), China's ultimate governing body.

Most PSC members hold both party and state positions. Hu Jintao is general secretary of the CCP's Central Committee and chairman of its Central Military Commission, for example, and president of the PRC and chairman of the PRC Central Military Commission. Similarly Wen Jiabao is the party's group secretary of the State Council and premier (also known as "prime minister") of the State Council (the Cabinet). The premier (head of government) is officially nominated by the president, and is formally appointed by the annual National People's Congress, China's parliament. In practice the appointment is in the gift of the Politburo.

There is no official pecking order of China's leaders, but there is usually a "protocol" ranking that can be deduced from the seating positions at meetings, and space devoted to and order of mention in the official media.

Business people watch protocol rankings avidly, because any change may herald a change of policy, which could in turn pose threats to a business or business model, or create new opportunities. There is also intense interest in the individuals who are moving up and down the rankings, because their backgrounds and connections could provide clues about their policy inclinations. Take President Hu's vision of a "harmonious society" that cares for the poor. It could have been, and almost certainly was, deduced from the fact that Hu came into the party through the Communist Youth League, one of the two main CCP factions, consisting largely of officials from poorer rural areas. A policy shift of this kind would have seemed likely after Hu replaced Jiang Zemin, because the latter's power base was the other main faction, the Shanghai coalition, which favors more market liberalization.

Those adept at reading the policy runes inscribed by the ebbs and flows of power in Chinese politics are very conscious of the importance of one particular institution. In addition to the two main factions of the CCP, there is also the Tsinghua Circle, a group of leading politicians who graduated from Beijing's Tsinghua University. Tsinghua, which will be celebrating its centenary in 2011, is one of China's leading universities. Its motto is "Self-discipline and social commitment," and it describes itself as being dedicated to academic excellence, the well-being of Chinese society, and global development. Members of the Tsinghua Circle are thought to hold tentatively pro-democratic views. They include three PSC members: PRC president Hu Jintao, vice-president Xi Jinping (see below), who is expected to succeed Hu as president and party leader in 2012, and Wu Bangguo, the head of the National People's Congress. Other circle members include a former president, Zhu Rhongji, a former vice-president, Huang Ju, and governor of the People's Bank of China, Zhou Xiaochuan.

Some members studied in the United States after graduating from Tsinghua, and some are believed to sympathize with the ideas of Hu Yaobang (1915–89), the now popular economic and political reformer, whose rehabilitation in recent years is seen by analysts as indicating that the current administration wants to associate itself with him. Like Premier Hu Jintao, Hu Yaobang came up through the Communist Youth League. He was also a patron of the current president in that he arranged for Hu Jintao's promotion to the CCP Central Office. Although he is not a member, Premier Wen Jiabo associated himself with the Tsinghua Circle when, on April 15, 2010 (the 21st anniversary of Hu's death) he contributed an article to *People's Daily*, "Recalling Hu Yaobang when I return to Xingyi." It was an account of an investigation he and Hu had conducted in 1986 into the lives of ordinary people in Xingyi county. It was not an overtly political piece, but much was made of it, and read into it, in the blogosphere.

The influence of the Tsinghua Circle and the rehabilitation of Hu Yaobang seem likely to survive the change of government in 2012.

The next president

Xi Jinping is heir presumptive to state president and CCP general secretary Hu Jintao. He was born in June 1953 in Beijing, but is by Chinese convention a native of Fuping county, Shanxi. He is the youngest son of the veteran Communist guerrilla leader Xi Zhongxun, who was head of the CCP's propaganda department when his son was born, and was later vice-chairman of the National People's Congress. When Xi was 10, his father was "purged," sent to work in a factory in Luoyang, and later jailed in 1968, during the Cultural Revolution. In 1969 Xi went to work in Yanchuan county, Shanxi, as part of Mao Zedong's Socialist Re-education program. While there he joined the Communist Youth League in 1971, and the CCP in 1974. By the time he left at the age of 22 he was party branch secretary of the production team. When asked years later on state television about this period of his life, Xi said, "It was emotional. It was a mood. And when the ideals of the Cultural Revolution could not be realized, it proved an illusion ...." What memories lay behind these words? A young man whose father was in jail, inspired by the dream of purifying society and purging the "four olds"—old ideas, old culture, old customs, old habits—only to find the brave hopes of youth turn to the ashes of burned books, violence, and vandalism.

Xi is not alone among the PRC's next generation of leaders to have dreamed such dreams in his youth, and to have experienced the pain and anguish of divided loyalties and disillusionment.

After returning to Beijing, Xi went to Tsinghua University to study chemical engineering, and is thus, like Hu Jintao, a member of both the Tsinghua Circle and the Youth League faction. He gained vital military experience during his three years serving as secretary to the vice premier and general secretary of the Central Military Commission (CMC), and subsequently served as an increasingly senior local government and party official in several provinces. He became governor of Fujian province in 2000, where his success in attracting investment from Taiwan was noted. Economic performance is an important criterion for judging the abilities of provincial governors and party chiefs.

In 2002 Xi moved to Zhejiang province where he was party chief for three years, during which time the provincial economy grew at 14 percent a year. His hard line on corruption in Zhejiang attracted national attention, and led to his appointment as alternate member of the 15th CCP Central Committee.

Xi's arrival on the national stage was confirmed in September 2006 by his appointment as party chief of Shanghai, the most important regional post in China, after the dismissal of Chen Liangyu in the wake of a social security fund scandal. For the first time in his 20-year marriage he had become better known in China than his wife, the folk singer Peng Liyuan. He became heir apparent to President Hu at the 2007 National Party Congress, when he was promoted to the PSC and later named vice-president.

What was perceived by some observers as a set-back in Xi's rise to power occurred in September 2009 at the Fourth Plenum of the CCP's 17th Central Committee, when he was not appointed vice-chairman of the CMC. The title has previously been an essential part of the heir presumptive's portfolio, but it may be that the appointment was simply delayed, or that the CCP is changing its leadership succession system. Xi was reported to have written to President Hu saying he did not want the job, because he needed to "focus on tasks at hand."

In addition to being PRC first vice president, Xi is also the principal of the Central Party School (see below), another key position previously held by Hu Jintao, Hua Gofeng, and Mao Zedong.

Among Xi's strengths as heir apparent are his connections. He came up through the Youth League, he is a Tsinghua graduate, and during his time as Shanghai party chief he forged links with the Shanghai Coalition. He is seen as favoring market-based economic reforms, being hard on corruption, and as indicated by a number of speeches since his anointment as crown prince, being interested in climate change issues. Less clear is the influence on his personal outlook of his revolutionary hero father, purged three times by Mao Zedong and one of the few CCP leaders to support the now rehabilitated Hu Yaobang (see above) during his lifetime.

The next premier

Another rising CCP star who was promoted to the PSC at the 2007 National Party congress is Li Keqiang. His appointment as first vice-premier is taken to indicate that he will succeed Wen Jiabao as premier. He is two years younger than Xi, and his father, a local official in Anhui province, is less illustrious. He is a long-time protégé of President Hu, however, and was once seen as Xi's rival for the top job.

During the Cultural Revolution he was sent to work on a collective farm in Fengyang county, Anhui where he joined the CCP, became the party head of the production team, and was declared the Outstanding Individual in the Study of Mao Zedong Thought.

He studied Law at Peking University, where he received his LLB and became the president of the university's Student Council. He later gained a doctorate in economics. He became Communist Youth League (CYL) secretary at Peking University in 1980, and joined the CYL's top leadership in 1982 as a member of its secretariat. This became Li's power base in the CCP, and led to his close relationship with Hu Jintao, who had also risen through the ranks of the CYL. He was the CYL's general secretary from 1993 to 1998.

Li became China's youngest governor when appointed the governor of Henan in June 1998 at the age of 43. His decision, in view of the serious corruption problem in the province, to leave his family in Beijing and live in Zhengzhou alone was noted and approved of, as was his refusal to accept invitations to banquets and other lavish events unconnected with government.

He is credited with transforming the relatively poor inland region into an attractive area for investment. He traveled all over the province identifying problems and looking for large-scale, rather than piecemeal solutions. In the early 1990s Henan was 28th in the national output rankings. By the time Li left Henan in 2004 it had risen to 18th.

Li moved to become CCP committee secretary in Liaoning in December 2004, where he is known for the "Five points and one line" road link project, which connected Dalian and Dandong and other smaller ports.

Li is married to Cheng Hong, a professor at Peking University, and daughter of a former vice-secretary of the CYL Central Committee.

CCP watchers, including businesses, will be on the look-out during the run up to the 2012 National Party Congress for signs that the balance of power in the PSC is gradually shifting from Hu and Wen, who want to maintain the current policy momentum, to Xi and Li, who want to initiate some of the changes of policy and policy emphasis that they are planning to implement when they assume the reins of power in 2012.

The Central Party School

"Where can you find the most careful drivers in China?" Answer: in one particular suburb in west Beijing where the next passer-by may be a future general secretary of the CCP and a PRC president. The joke refers to the campus of the Party School of the CCP's Central Committee, more commonly known as the Central Party School (CPS). This is where the CCP trains all high-ranking officials, including provincial party chiefs, governors, ministers, and generals. Newly appointed mid-ranking officials must also take courses at the CPS for periods ranging from three months to three years.

Two decades ago, when the school was classified as a "confidential unit," careless drivers would have been unaware of the risks they were running, because the CPS was not identified on maps or entered in any directories. Security is still very tight, but the school is more open now.

The curriculum includes Marxism-Leninism, Mao Zedong Thought, Deng Xiaoping Theory, and CCP principles, as well as western political theories, economics, law, religion, science and technology, and military matters. A decade ago the school ran classes on history and geography, but improved general education levels in China made these superfluous, and they have been replaced by classes on other subjects, including opera appreciation and diplomatic etiquette. There are also practical seminars on challenges that students have encountered at work, such as how to increase rural incomes, attract new investment to finance local development, and combat corruption.

China also sends its officials to study abroad. Since 2002 some 60 CPS students have been sent each year to attend the Kennedy School of Government's two-month public administration program at Harvard University, for example.

At any one time the school has some 1,300 students on campus, most chosen by the Organization Department of the CCP Central Committee and its provincial and municipal departments. Since 2002, when the 16th National Party Congress decided to allow private entrepreneurs to join the party, the CPS's education and training programs have also been open to private-sector business people.

The discipline is tight and the regimen is rigorous. Absences from class are not permitted without good reason, school administrators are in charge of leave, and anyone returning after 11 pm must sign in at the reception desk. Alarm clocks in the dormitories are set for 7.30 am, and unruly behavior in class could bring a promising political career to a premature end.

There is a special program for young and middle-aged officials which usually lasts a year, to which the Organization Department of the CCP's Central Committee sends staff to sit in on discussions, and identify potential high-flyers. About a third of these students are subsequently promoted to positions of leadership at provincial or ministerial level.

The CPS incorporates the Training Centre of the State-owned Assets Supervision and Administration Commission (SASAC), which owns, and is charged with modernizing and restructuring, China's central state-owned enterprises (SOEs), to whom it appoints senior executives. The Training Centre is a branch of the CPS, but under the control of the SASAC. It organizes and conducts the education and training of SASAC officials and SOE executives (see Chapter 6).

Brainstorming sessions attended by top CCP leaders are held at the CPS on the eve of every major policy shift, and since 1992 senior party officials have delivered speeches at the school before every National Party Congress and the announcement of significant policy changes.

Another indication of the great importance the CCP attaches to the school is the fact that the CPS presidency is a major step towards China's highest office. The current PRC president and CCP general secretary, Hu Jintao, was the CPS president from 1993 to 2002, and his heir apparent, Xi Jinping, has been CPS president since 2007.

Global institutions are also aware of the school's importance, and the elevated destinies of some of its students. When Angel Gurría, secretary-general of the Organisation for Economic Co-operation and Development (OECD), delivered a speech at the school on March 23, 2010, on "The OECD, the world economy and China," he knew that his audience probably included people who would decide whether or not China's current Enhanced Engagement relationship with the OECD would blossom into full membership.

The CPS is a formidable political instrument. Its pedagogic aim is to align the identities and beliefs of students, at every level and in every province and region, with those of the Party centre. This helps to endow China's system of government with a deep structure of shared beliefs and common understandings, which in turn creates a stable administrative and regulatory environment.

Foreign firms operating in China would do well to be aware of this important institution, and might even consider taking some courses at the CPS to learn about current government thinking, and to make contact with the next generation of leaders.

The People's Liberation Army

The CMCs control the PRC's People's Liberation Army (PLA), which includes the army, navy, and airforce. China's 2.3 million strong army is the world's largest, followed by the United States with 1.4 million, India with 1.3 million, and Russia with 1.2 million.

Nominal control is in the hands of the CMC of the People's Republic of China (the "state CMC"), answerable to the Standing Committee of the National People's Congress, which elects its chairman, who is, ex officio, commander-in-chief of the PLA. In reality, however, command and control of the PLA is in the hands of the CMC of the CCP Central Committee (the "party CMC"). Since the membership of both CMCs is identical, the distinction is academic in practice.

Although the chairman of the CMC is usually head of state and general secretary of the party, as is currently the case, this is not set in stone. Deng Xiaoping and Jiang Zemin both retained their positions as CMC chairman after retiring as president and CCP general secretary.

An unusual feature of the PLA is that, until the mid-1990s at any rate, it was a very wealthy organization with extensive commercial interests, particularly in real estate. This was a legacy of the 1950s and 1960s when the PLA, seeking financial and material self-sufficiency within an inefficient state-owned system, bought farms, opened guest houses, and built factories to support its own needs. Following Deng Xiaoping's economic reforms, some of these ventures became very profitable. Many guest houses, for example, which were originally designed for recreation for military personnel were converted into hotels.

With an estimated 20,000 firms at one time, ranging from munitions factories to Baskin-Robbins ice cream franchises, "PLA Inc." as it was sometimes dubbed was one of the largest commercial concerns in China.

Party officials became concerned about the PLA's growing portfolio of businesses in the early 1990s for three reasons. It was seen to be adversely affecting the PLA's military readiness, it encouraged corruption, and it provided the military with an independent source of income that could undermine its loyalty to the party. CCP leaders had long been concerned about such a danger. "Power comes from the barrel of the gun," Mao Zedong had said. "Our principle is that the party controls the gun, and the gun must never be allowed to control the party."

A program was accordingly launched to convert the PLA's business enterprises into private companies managed by former PLA officers, and to change military procurement from a system in which the PLA had direct control over its sources of supply, to a system similar to those of western countries. This spin-off of PLA businesses was largely complete by the end of 2000. It was not controversial. The PLA's senior officers are not thought to have raised any objections, and the PLA remains an important part of the system.

The system of government

China's system of government is organized along federal lines, much as it was in imperial times. There is a central, guiding CCP mind in Beijing that determines general direction, issues instructions, and distributes information through a hierarchy of local party and government institutions. Decision are made centrally, but executed locally.

It is not, of course, quite as simple as that. China's governance system has been described as "fragmented authoritarianism."[1] According to this model separate state and party institutions and bureaucracies seek consensus on policies, through bargaining and negotiation. When consensus cannot be achieved, conflict ensues and each group "lobbies" for its own policy. More "fragments," in the form of provincial and municipal institutions, were brought into the system during the great decentralization of the 1980s, and it has been suggested that an additional interest group, in the form of private business people, is in the process of complicating the system even further.

The party and government, although officially separate, are almost totally fused in practice. Party members hold almost all official posts, at every level, and the education and training of officials at central and local levels is in the hands of party institutions, such as

Box 5.1 Yuan Yafei

Chairman of HTSB

Yuan Yafei with cigar
Source: Luyang Jiang

Yuan Yafei, founder of the HTSB group, the business interests of which range from chain stores and manufacturing to finance and real estate, puffed deeply on his Cohiba cigar and announced, "I'm a dictator."

"Are you sure you want to say that?" one of us asked.

"Well, at least I'm being honest," he replied.

Yuan believes that, to create a family spirit in his business, he needs to "control the minds" of his 15,000 employees. He grew up in a military family. He manages his group like an army and each business as an army division. His military-style *Dong Ban* (personal support team), from which new initiatives and decisions are issued, consists of several assistants who keep him in contact with each business. One is on hand day and night to record his ideas, and an administration department manages his schedule.

The vice presidents (VPs), most of whom have either doctorates or Master's degrees from foreign universities, are the chiefs of staff. They form the Vice Presidents Group, and are supported by a team of professional statisticians. They are responsible for gathering and analyzing data on operating company performance, competitors, and other key variables to enable Yuan to make well-informed decisions.

The heads of the four industry sectors supply information to the relevant assistants and the VP group, but report directly to Yuan. He is the commander. The VPs act as a think-tank and communications hub.

All senior managers are required to write reports each month criticizing their performances and identifying what needs to be improved. "I need to know what they're thinking," says Yuan. "I get an idea what's on their minds from their reports, and send back my comments by email."

Yuan is deeply interested in business types and models, and styles of management. He believes the entrepreneurial, as opposed to the managerial, spirit can be passed on, not only from generation to generation, but also by employees within an enterprise. It requires constant negation and conquering of the self, but can help to sustain a company's success as long as it conforms with the social and economic spirits of the time.

The essence of a family-owned enterprise is responsibility, as Yuan sees it. It also requires a professional attitude, but not necessarily professional know-how, so that the company can employ professional managers when necessary. He believes that the stability provided by a professional attitude is crucial for Chinese companies. None of Yuan's relatives work for his company. He says it would be unfair to other employees in the first place, and second, he has no relatives with competitive work advantages. In his view a family enterprise acts as a family, but he sees himself as more like his employees' godfather.

"I have no partners," says Yuan, emphasizing the point with a gesture and a cloud of cigar smoke. "I only have employees. A partner shares the same values. Fortune is an honor for a businessman. No employee has that perception of money." He started HSTB in 1994 with initial capital of 20,000 yuan. Its total assets are now worth 20 billion yuan.

Yuan is involved in three kinds of company. Where he has operational control he acts like an emperor and controls minds, culture, and management. Where he is a purely financial investor, but his partners have operational control, he only reads the financial statements and makes strategies. Where he mainly focuses on returns on investment, he has no involvement in the management.

Yuan is going his own way with his emperor model of management, but he is not too proud to learn from the West. He admires the business models of three American companies in particular: Walmart, for its one-shop-for-everything philosophy, McDonald's, for its standardization, and Dell for its "no inventory" principle.

Luyang Jiang and the author

the CPS (see above). This fusion of party and state is evident at the highest level—the state president is always the party's general secretary—and is exemplified by the fact that the membership of the CMC of the PRC (a state body) is identical to that of the CMC of the CCP (a party body—see above).

Through its ownership and use of the Xinhua news agency, CCTV, and *People's Daily*, the CCP has become adept at influencing and guiding public opinion, testing new policies, and gathering support for and implementing new priorities and policy directions. At present, for example, everyone knows that the CCP/government is taking a hard line against local corruption and unethical business practices, is eager to reduce pollution, and has a long-term desire to create a more "harmonious society," which is known to mean reducing the growing disparity between urban and rural incomes. It has also got its timing right. China was "ready" for the Olympics in 2008 and for Expo in 2010, and it is ready now, in terms of the country's technological capabilities, to "clean up" its industries and local administrations in both senses of the term.

The state-owned media are generally trusted by the people, because they are state-owned and thus have no commercial axes to grind, or partisan political positions to adopt. "Media in China have a high trust level," says CCTV-2 director Guo Zhenxi. "In the West, there are more sources of information, but less trust" (see page 58).

The role of the state-owned media as generally trusted information channels for government makes them required reading and watching for foreign and domestic business people. Those who are most adept at analyzing articles and reported speeches, and deducing changes in "protocol" rankings from pictures and orders of mention, have a significant competitive advantage over their rivals.

The Chinese people generally comply with the light hand of central direction. New slogans developed to promote new CCP priorities are repeated constantly in the state-owned media and speeches, and are heeded. For example, the idea that salary freezes rather than lay-offs were the most appropriate way to deal with the fall-out from the global financial crisis originated with the party centre, and was widely accepted within a month.

There are many thousands of incidents of civil unrest each year in China, but the opposition they represent is for example against municipal and local administrators for perceived violations of property rights (so-called "land grabs") rather than against central government. By and large, the people trust the government, and are in agreement with its priorities and policy directions.

For westerners, among the most distinctive features of the Chinese system of government is the glacial pace at which China's colossal ship of state changes course. Because the consequences of a policy mistake affecting 1.3 billion people can be so horrendous (witness the famine following the Great Leap Forward), China's leaders do not do anything abruptly, or without considering all of the angles and trying to anticipate all the unintended side-effects

When everything else is changing all the time, the government is a voice of calm, and a source of stability. It takes the long view. Because it has no need to renew its mandate to govern every five years or so, it can afford to approach its goals slowly, step by step, feeling the shape and texture of each stone as it crosses the river.

Democracy is a case in point. It is not inconceivable that China will move towards a multi-party democracy within the next 30 years, but it will not happen overnight, and will not be effected by sudden constitutional reform. The Chinese way is step, by step, with each proposed step informally leaked to elicit responses. The brain-storming sessions at the CPS, which are attended by party leaders (see above), are just one example of the numerous informal policy-testing processes that precede changes in the government's emphases and priorities.

It might, for example, become apparent in retrospect that the recent rehabilitation of the political reformer Hu Yaobang, with whose views the Tsinghua Circle are said to sympathize (see above), was such a step. The direct elections for municipal Party officials at four government units in Shenzhen in April 2010 might be another. (Direct elections had previously been confined to village councils and local People's Congresses.) The *Shenzhen Daily* reported that Huang Ligui, former assistant to the president of Skyworth Group, a successful Shenzhen electronics company, became the first deputy to a Party Congress to be chosen by a direct election in Shenzhen on April 9. Direct elections for another three posts were held the following week. It was billed as part of a pilot program of intra-Party democracy, which followed indirect elections of candidates for Shenzhen bureau chief seats in May 2008. It may prove to have no long-term significance. It is hard to believe, however, that the Party centre was unaware of and did not sanction the experiment.

The long time-horizons of government and the incremental, step-by-step approach to policy shifts clearly have important implications for businesses operating in China. They create a stability in the legislative and regulatory environments that is rare in countries where policy changes are the currency political parties use to buy votes every few years. The reduction in the risk that markets will be undermined or business models compromised by policy shifts is a boon for China's merchants, but it is offset by their lack of overt access to and influence over the policy-making process.

Now that several million private entrepreneurs are CCP members the influence of the business lobby on the government's legislative and regulatory actions may begin to increase. For the time being, however, government in modern China plays a role in the lives of China's merchants very similar to the role it played in the age of the emperors. It cannot be directed. China's merchants know they can only accommodate it, and adapt to it. Like the weather, it is a given. It is the *Dao*; the land.

As the owner of land, the government has a very material influence on the Chinese way of doing business. When private entrepreneurs require more land for development, they apply to central and local governments for three or four times as much as they need, knowing that constantly rising prices will enable them to sell the surplus at a considerable profit. It is an adaptation to an environment in which tradable land is in short supply, and acts as a form of free risk management; if a business fails, the entrepreneur will still have the property profits. Zhang Yong, chairman of Haidilao Hotpot Company (see page 69), is very unusual in this respect, because he rents, rather than buys his property.

This is a brief summary of the governance environment within which a distinctively Chinese style of management is emerging. The third sculptor of the Chinese management style is the engine of economic development itself, China's entrepreneurial spirit.

Summary

- The events of May 4, 1919 heralded the birth of modern China.
- Reading the policy runes and protocol rankings is an essential part of effective environmental scanning.
- Xi Jinping and Li Keqiang are expected to become president and premier respectively in 2012.
- The Central Party School helps to align the beliefs of party members and government officials with those of the Party centre.
- China's governance system has been described as "fragmented authoritarianism."
- The CCP is adept at influencing and guiding public opinion through the state-owned media.
- The people trust the central government.

Note

1 Kenneth Lieberthal and Michel Oksenberg (1988) *Policy Making in China: Leaders, Structures, and Processes*, New Haven, Conn.: Princeton University Press.

CHAPTER 6

Energy

Trade and industry emerge, spontaneously, from the simple logic of the human condition; from the need for food, shelter, and warmth, from the ability to manipulate and add value, and from differences in skills, know-how, and resources. Adam Smith explained that while animals fend for themselves:

> Among men ... the most dissimilar geniuses are of use to one another; the different products of their respective talents, by the general disposition to truck, barter, and exchange, being brought, as it were, into a common stock, where every man may purchase whatever part of the produce of other men's talents he has occasion for.[1]

The motivation for engaging in trade, a desire for wealth, is just as old and just as natural, according to Max Weber:

> The impulse to acquisition, pursuit of gain, of money ... has in itself nothing to do with capitalism. This impulse exists and has existed among waiters, physicians, coachmen, artists, prostitutes, dishonest officials, soldiers, nobles, crusaders, gamblers and beggars ... it has been common to all sorts...of men, at all times and in all countries of the earth, wherever the ... possibility of it is or has been given.[2]

Salt and stone may have been the first "traded" goods. The Chinese are thought to have traded salt made by boiling brine in pans of saline soil from desert basins more than 4,000 years ago.

For a long time it was merchants rather than craftspeople (people who made things) who dominated economic activity. Ships and caravans carrying goods to and fro along trade routes such as the Silk Road generated wealth in a system known as mercantilism, which reached its high point in the fifteenth and sixteenth centuries, but was still much in evidence in the eighteenth century. It was a "mercantilist" dispute about trading rights that led to the Opium Wars in China in the mid-nineteenth century (see Chapter 9).

Mercantilism embraced the principles of private property, and used markets to coordinate economic activity. But its focus was on the interests of the sovereign or the state, rather than on individual owners of economic resources. The concern of states, during the mercantilist era, was to accumulate wealth in the form of gold and silver through trade.

Mercantilism evolved into capitalism, and "merchants" were replaced by "entrepreneurs" as the primary economic agents, when it became clear that the real wealth of any nation was not its hoard of gold and silver, but its ability to produce goods and services.

This transformation occurred initially in England, during a sudden burst of entrepreneurial activity in the eighteenth century, known as the Industrial Revolution, driven by technological advances such as the substitution of coal for charcoal in iron smelting—achieved in China in the eleventh century—and Watt's invention of the external condenser steam engine.

Such sudden bursts of entrepreneurial activity in different places at different times have created the modern world. England in the eighteenth century; the opening-up of the American west by railroads; the birth of the automobile industry and mass production techniques in Detroit, in America's Midwest; the microelectronics revolution in Silicon Valley on America's west coast; the "dot.com" revolution in cyberspace; and the dramatic burst of entrepreneurial activity in the final quarter of the twentieth century that turned China from an isolated and inefficient bastion of state corporatism into a great economic power.

In an article in *China Entrepreneur* in 2009, Fu Guoyong traced the origins of China's "entrepreneurial" tradition—as opposed to the ancient merchant tradition from which it emerged—back to the end of the nineteenth century. He pointed out that between 1872 and 1894 only 72 new enterprises were incorporated in China, and all were either merchant-run or government-run or government supervised. From 1895, when Zhang Jian incorporated Dasheng Cotton

Mill, to 1913, 549 new enterprises were incorporated, almost a quarter of which were what Fu calls "new-style enterprises" run by entrepreneurs. In addition to Zhang, China's early entrepreneur heroes also included the Rong Brothers (silk, flour, and cotton milling), Mu Ouchu (cotton), Zhou Xuexi (mining, cement), Fan Xudong (chemicals), Lu Zuofu (shipping and social reform), Liu Hongsheng (cement, matches), Yu Qiaqing (transport), and Chen Guangfu (1880–1976, also known as K. P. Chen—banking, travel, insurance).[3]

Fu argues that men such as these brought to China the "spirits" of "exploration, exploitation, and innovation" that the traditional Chinese culture had lacked, but that they were different from the early western entrepreneurs of the seventeenth and eighteenth centuries in having a social conscience and in seeing their activities as contributing to the strength of China as a whole. Some westerners will disagree, and may point, for example, to the similarities between Lu Zuofu's social experiments and those of the Cadbury chocolate dynasty in England. There is little evidence, however, that the early western entrepreneurs harbored nationalist feelings similar to those felt by Fu's entrepreneurs: namely, that they were "developing industry and commerce to save China" or "saving China by improving people's living standard," or "saving China by cotton and iron." Whether or not such sentiments reflected the fact that the entrepreneurs were active during China's so-called "century of humiliation," it seems clear that the idea that entrepreneurs contribute to the health of society at large, and to the strength of the country as a whole, is deeply embedded in China's entrepreneurial culture.

Entrepreneurial drive

What is this entrepreneurial energy that has changed the course of history, and under what conditions does it flourish?

The American economist Israel Kirzner tried to integrate a quality he calls "entrepreneurial alertness" into economic theory, and said that although it is hard to measure or make a market in, it is best seen as the fourth factor of production alongside land, labor, and capital.[4]

The belief that entrepreneurs embody a scarce economic resource is shared by one of China's most illustrious entrepreneurs, Ma Yun

—better known by his westernized name, Jack Ma—who argues in his speeches that the scarce resource is not money, but entrepreneurial spirit, dreams, and values (see below).

Kirzner said that "entrepreneurial alertness" was an aspect of cultural vision—an optical sensing system that is constantly scanning the business environment for what he called "concatenations of events, realized or prospective, which offer pure gain." Tom Peters, the American management writer, put the same point in another way that conveyed the strangeness of this entrepreneurial "sense."[5] He said that entrepreneurship is "unreasonable conviction, based on inadequate evidence." But, of course, for the entrepreneur, the conviction is not unreasonable, and the evidence is not inadequate.

Kirzner's "entrepreneurial alertness" resembles the idea that good fortune is enjoyed by those who look for it. This was demonstrated by an intriguing experiment. Subjects were divided into two groups depending on whether they saw themselves as lucky or unlucky. Both groups were asked to look at the same magazine, and say as soon as they could how many advertisements it contained. The "lucky" group responded much faster than the other group, because most had seen and read a half-page advertisement on page 2, which consisted of the words "there are 15 advertisements in this magazine."

As we saw in Chapter 4, luck and fate both play important roles in Chinese culture, through the influence of the *I Ching* and Daoism. The Chinese, like the Americans, have a positive attitude to risk, which is a quality characteristic of entrepreneurs. Entrepreneurs are optimists. In business there is no such person as a successful pessimist.

Another quality characteristic of entrepreneurs is that they do not take things for granted. For them, the world is malleable. Things do not have to be the way they are. They can be changed by acts of will. This belief that the individual is actively involved in the creation of tomorrow's world is more plausible, and so more widely held, at some times, and in some circumstances, than others.

It is more common, for instance, at the beginnings of developments and trends; in what might be called a "frontier" environment. This was the lesson of the *I Ching* (see Chapter 4). The Book of Changes became a book of wisdom when the original system of divination was augmented with the idea that change is controllable to some extent in its early, germinal stage.

Entrepreneurialism flourished during the taming of America's "wild west," for example; following the invention of internal combustion and semiconductors; after the cracking of the genetic code; after the internet became a mass market medium. During the first three decades of the People's Republic of China (PRC), entrepreneurs were thin on the ground, or rather mostly underground. When Deng Xiaoping opened China, and announced it was "glorious to be rich," entrepreneur-run enterprises sprang up all over China like flowers in spring. In frontier environments, business landscapes are full of empty niches waiting to be spotted by alert entrepreneurs, and occupied.

It has been suggested that a second frontier for entrepreneurs may open up in China over the next few years, as the wealth created in the cities gradually diffuses into rural areas. The usual pattern of economic development is for enterprises to satisfy the domestic market first, and then export. It looks as if it will be the other way round in China.

At other times when the frontiers have reached the sea and most of the niches in the business ecosystem have been occupied, there is less scope for entrepreneurs, and if the enterprises they founded prosper, there will come a time when they feel that they have more to protect than to gain.

A story was told, in the late 1980s, about two men standing on the roof of a New York skyscraper, looking down at a cortege of black limousines moving slowly down a street below. "Has someone famous died?" asked one. "No" said the other. "That's IBM's lawyers going to lunch." IBM was at the height of its powers at the time, but as the story indicated, it was devoting enormous amounts of time and resources to protecting its then dominant position in the computer market. A high-tech company that spends more on lawyers' fees than on research and development has surely, it was suggested, lost its pioneering, entrepreneurial spirit.

What was one to make, therefore, of the news in April 2010 that aigo, one of China's most successful electronics groups, had filed lawsuits to block sales of some Hewlett-Packard and Toshiba laptop computers, alleging violation of aigo's USB Plus adaptor patents? Was this a sign that aigo was running out of growth opportunities, and saw money spent on protecting intellectual property it already possessed as better spent than money invested in developing new intellectual property? Or was it simply a gambit by aigo's founder and chief executive, Feng Jun (see page 114), in the great game of business? It would be up to the courts to determine the merits of the case. But a claim by a Chinese company that two pillars of the computer-making establishment were violating its patent rights was sure to be widely reported in the western press (there was a half-page article on aigo in the *Financial Times* of London a week after the lawsuits were filed), would speak volumes about the quality of aigo's technology, and might be seen more generally as a sign that the flows of technology between China and more developed economies were becoming two-way.

If this was part of Feng's motivation for filing the lawsuits, and the fact that the word "aigo" is Chinese for "patriot" suggests it may have been, it would indicate that the belief noted above among early "new-style" Chinese entrepreneurs that they were "developing industry and commerce to save China" survives today.

Feng was 40 at the time the lawsuits were filed, and thus unlikely to be running out of entrepreneurial energy. He is also fond of the "business as a game" metaphor, and has suggested modifying the game of western chess by introducing four additional major pieces; a pair of cannon (*pao*) each side from the Chinese version of chess known as Xiangqi.

Whatever the motivation for the aigo lawsuits, there is concern in some quarters that China may indeed be losing its entrepreneurial edge. Qin Shuo, editor in chief of *China Business News* (*CBN*), is worried that what he calls China's "entrepreneur drive" might be weakened or blunted by success. He cites the "drive theory" of the American psychologist Clark Hull (1884–1952), who argued that drive emerges from need. Organisms suffer deprivation, deprivation creates need, and needs motivate the organisms to pursue goals that reduce those needs. In other words, as Shuo says, "When needs are satisfied, the tension disappears and drive is reduced."[6] He said

Box 6.1 Feng Jun

CEO of Beijing Huaqi Information

Feng Jun with Cannon
Source: Luyang Jiang

Feng Jun is a showman. He does not speak much English, but during a break on a business television show shortly before the Beijing Olympics in 2008, he urged the audience to practice English with him. He is one of the most successful and the least self-conscious of the current generation of Chinese entrepreneurs. He is always promoting either his company, Huaqi, or its aigo brand products, and never tires of demonstrating the latter, especially to foreigners.

"When do you find the time to manage?" we asked.

"I love my company," he said. "I love my products."

When he graduated from Tsinghua University in 1992 he was assigned to Beijing Construction Engineering Company, but left when he knew the company would send him to Malaysia. He did not go abroad as did many of his contemporaries. Inspired by the speech Deng Xiaoping delivered in Shenzhen during his southern tour (see Chapter 1), he went to Zhong Guan Cun Science Park (Z-Park) in Beijing with 260 yuan in his pocket, and started selling computer keyboards.

He thinks he was lucky to have been born in 1969, and to have just graduated when Deng launched his reforms. "If Bill Gates, or Steve Jobs had been born a year earlier, or a year later, they might not have achieved what they did," he says. "I was lucky to be born when I was. Everything came together; the timing, the location, and the environment—the government was encouraging young people to start businesses."

Feng's original nickname in the Chinese PC industry was "five yuan Feng," after he cut his profit margin on PC keyboards from the 50 yuan industry standard to 5 yuan. He now prefers "six wins Feng," after his articulation of a new "stakeholder" model that committed Huaqi to reconciling the interests of six interested parties: "the public" (existing and prospective customers), "agencies" (Huaqi's distributors), Huaqi employees, the company, suppliers, and society at large.

Feng sees business in terms of principles, models, and images, such as his "six wins" principle; the 1+1=11 idea, which symbolizes the synergistic value creation when two parties are moving to the same destination from different starting points; and what he calls the aigo "chess culture," which symbolizes teamwork and synergies that emerge from blending the cultures of the East and West.

Feng's chess board has 36 pieces—the 32 from international chess and two pairs of cannon from Chinese chess. When asked which piece he is, he grins and says he could be any of them, apart from the queen. He is really the king, of course (in that he grasps the big picture and provides inspirational management). He began as a knight, and was often on the defensive. Feng believes in collaboration, mixing cultures, and changing the game. "You take the good parts of each, and make them work together," he says. Feng sees aigo as the cannon (which combines intelligence and creativity to attain great achievement).

He likens the relationship between "stability" and "efficiency" to the relationship between pyramids and skyscrapers. He approves of the pyramid, which increases its height while strengthening its base. "During the initial stage companies should develop at a steady pace, take into account the interests of all related parties, and help everyone to grow. Only when the foundations are solid enough should we consider building skyscrapers on top of the pyramids."

Luyang Jiang and the author

that over the past 30 years, most of China's entrepreneurs "have accumulated enough wealth to achieve financial freedom and a much higher social status," but had forgotten the deprivation that had originally driven them to "stand behind the counter during the day and sleep on the floor at night."

A 2008 survey of southeastern coastal areas found that the rate of company start-ups had fallen significantly in the previous two years. Li Lan, secretary general of the China Entrepreneur Survey System, told a similar story for China as a whole, at the National People's Congress in March, 2009.

The idea that deprivation can create entrepreneurial drive was the theme of R. H. Tawney's *Religion and the Rise of Capitalism*,[7] which explored the relationship between nonconformist Protestantism and economic development in the sixteenth and seventeenth centuries in England. The reason that nonconformists, particularly the Quakers, played such a central role in the Industrial Revolution, according to Tawney, was that adherence to their beliefs deprived them of access to the political system. It was the exclusion from political institutions that drove them to seek success and self-esteem in entrepreneurial activity.

If there is any truth in this, it could be argued that the decision of the Chinese Communist Party (CCP) in 2002 to allow private sector entrepreneurs to join the party might have contributed to some extent to a diminution of China's "entrepreneur drive."

But as Shuo pointed out in his article, there are internal as well external factors at work. Why is it that some entrepreneurs remain driven while others lose their drive in the same environment? Shuo quotes the example of Li Dongsheng, president of TCL Corporation, who embarked on a major reconstruction of TCL's culture in 2006 in a program called Rebirth of the Eagle. Li explained:

> In a company's life cycle, sometimes we have to make tough decisions to start a renewal process. To fly again, we must abandon old, undesirable habits and traditions, and things that have contributed to our growth, but are now a barrier to our success. Such transformation is painful to the company, all the employees, and to me alike. But to ensure the survival of the company, and achieve our development goal, we must go through the ordeal!

As has been said, "You can't save a company that is doing well." If you don't have a crisis, you have to invent one.

Other entrepreneurs sustain their drive by reinventing themselves rather than their companies. Ji Qi, chief executive for the time being of Hanting Hotels, said: "The reason I keep starting up new businesses and traveling is that I want continuously to surpass myself, and tackle new challenges. I'm still so young, why would I stop?" His role model is Jim Clark, founder of SGI, Netscape, and Healtheon. "He has a unique orangutan philosophy," says Ji; "always jumping to another vine."

Shuo has two prescriptions for reviving China's entrepreneur drive—one external and one internal. He advocates further reform, less regulation, breaking up monopolies, more level playing fields to foster competition, and a socialist legal system, to match China's socialist market economy.

His internal prescription for entrepreneurs is humility. They have contributed substantially to China's economic growth over the past 30 years, but should acknowledge that their success is partly due to Deng Xiaoping's opening up. China's economic growth since 1978 has been rapid, and largely uninterrupted. "If they realize this historic upswing trend," Shuo says, "then the Chinese entrepreneurs would not take all the credit and ... become more sober and humble."

Although it is a Confucian virtue, humility is not a quality often found in entrepreneurs. And nor should it be expected. The humble entrepreneur is as much a contradiction in terms as the successful pessimist. Confucianism, with its distaste for brash individualism and the urge to make money and seek profit, is not a philosophy or way of life within which entrepreneurialism sits comfortably. That the Chinese have nonetheless come to treasure entrepreneurs and give them high social status is one of the most important legacies of the American experiment.

The entrepreneur as "merchant" has always had a respected place in Chinese society. The entrepreneur as a "superstar" of pop culture, as innovator, creator, and the architect of modern China, is new, and has important implications for the emerging Chinese management style. But these high-profile, private entrepreneurs are operating within a business culture to which other traditions and approaches are contributing.

Chinese businesses

To understand how these various business traditions and approaches are interacting to create a distinctively Chinese management style, it is useful to recall the distinctions made in Chapter 1, between public sector enterprises and three types of private enterprise.

Public sector

Central state-owned enterprises (SOEs) are large organizations run by party members close to the government, who are, to all intents and purposes, civil servants. With US$3.3 trillion worth of sales in 2009, and many millions of employees, they are politically as well as economically powerful, and protected from competition. Some are heavily subsidized. Since 2003, they have been owned by the State Assets Supervision and Administration Commission (SASAC), charged with restructuring and consolidating the state sector through the State Development and Investment Corp. The objective is to spin off the profitable SOEs and consolidate the rest into more focused businesses.

China's massive economic stimulus package in 2009, including large public infrastructure projects and substantial lending by state-owned banks, was widely criticized as favoring SOEs at the expense of private firms. The term encapsulating the sentiment was *guojin mintui* (the state advances and private companies retreat). Comments at a meeting of the 37th economic committee of the Chinese People's Political Consultative Conference (CPPCC) in March, 2010 suggested some SOE managers are becoming increasingly irritated by such comments, and by the less than flattering comparisons usually drawn between them and the high-profile private entrepreneurs.

Responding to criticisms by fellow delegate Zhang Shiping, of the All China Federation of Trade Unions, that SOE bosses earn 18 times as much as their front-line workers, Liu Deshu, the president of Sinochem Group, said, "Companies with the biggest difference between top executives and ordinary workers; it is absolutely not state-owned companies." Gesturing towards an empty seat, Liu said, "Today Yang Yuanqing [chief executive of private computer-maker, Lenovo, see pages 125–6] isn't here. If we asked … what his salary is compared with his workers' salaries, whose difference would be bigger?" Liu estimated Yang's pay was 36 million yuan ($5.3 million). "Among us who work for state-owned companies, who makes that much?"

Lenovo's annual report shows that Yang Yuanqing earned $7.23 million in 2009 including basic salary of $846,000, bonuses, share issues, and other compensation.

Other SOE bosses weighed in. Yang Kaisheng, head of the Industrial and Commercial Bank of China, questioned the accuracy of Zhang's "18 times" figure, and Sun Wenjie, chairman of China State Construction Engineering Corp., complained about the social responsibilities of SOEs and the fact that they were not allowed to invest in property.

The last was a telling point, because property investment is a key component of the business model employed by China's large private-sector enterprises (see Chapter 5). It is often their second wing as they soar like eagles on the updrafts from China's fast-growing economy. SOE leaders can only look enviously on, as they roar past on moon rockets powered by captive markets and government subsidy.

Yang was applauded by other SOE bosses when he said, "State-owned enterprise leaders are the leaders of their own companies, not the leaders of the country .... If I manage my company efficiently and fairly, that's enough." He urged other SOE bosses to:

> speak up and say a few things about state-owned companies. We are not trying to destroy this country. Last year, we were on the front lines! If it wasn't for our efforts GDP would have fallen down from the sky! We employ so many workers .... We are people, not gods!

The frustration of SOE bosses is understandable. They constitute a separate management tradition in China. They are appointed and can be fired by SASAC, they are trained separately in the SASAC branch of the CPS (see Chapter 5), and their management models and styles are governed by SASAC rules. They play the role of the "merchant," but they are actually members of the "administrator" class. It must be irksome for them that in a society in which many private-sector entrepreneurs have the status of heroes, because of their dynamism and efficiency, China's public sector is still regarded as a haven for inefficiency and stagnation.

Private sector

As in every economy, private enterprises vary enormously, but they have one quality in common—youth. In their present forms, at any rate, they are all 30 years old or younger. Many are still run by their founders, and are dealing with everything for the first time.

It is first time for a lot of things in China today: first-time car owner, first-time home owner, first-time make-up user, first-time manager, first-time entrepreneur. This is why the environment for business is so unpredictable and full of opportunity; and why the emerging Chinese management model should be seen as being still in the fetal stage, with plenty of development options still open to it.

As suggested in Chapter 1 it is useful to distinguish between three types of private enterprise—wholly indigenous, first or second-generation family SMEs, many of which began life as *qian dian, hou chang* (shop in front, factory behind) companies (see Chapter 1), sea-turtle firms, set up by entrepreneurs trained in Europe or the United States who believe "West is best" in management, and firms run by men and women, some of whom are sea-turtles, who believe that although "west may be best in the West," it is not so in China, and are running their firms without management textbooks, in ways that seem better suited to the Chinese environment.

It is easy to over-simplify here (there are successful examples of all three types), but by and large the first have emerged from the "merchant tradition" and tend to be dependent on maintaining good relationships with "administrators." The second are "alien" in the sense that they are trying to employ a western management model in the belief that it is the best management model available. They are more professionally run, but more prone to misjudge the market and make management mistakes, because they are insufficiently intimate with, or concerned about, the nuances of China's culture. The third are run by genuinely "Chinese" entrepreneurs, who acknowledge the necessity, but not the primacy of professionalism. They tend to be the most successful.

Vimicro Corp., run by John Deng (see page 122), illustrates how the categories merge into each other. At first, and to some extent at second, sight Vimicro looks like an archetypal sea-turtle company, with its professional management systems and stock options for key staff. But Deng differs from his counterparts in Silicon Valley in that he is passionately patriotic and feels he is contributing to the economic and industrial development of his country. It is hard to believe his sense of patriotic duty and "giving back" will have no impact on Vimicro's evolving culture and management style.

"Chinese" entrepreneurs

Western entrepreneurs and business leaders tend to "stick to their knitting." They talk about business and management, but rarely venture opinions on other subjects. Many of China's entrepreneurs talk openly and often about spirituality, philosophy, and morality, and how their values and management styles reflect and are aligned with China's culture and traditions. It is as if they feel a need in

Box 6.2 Zhonghan (John) Deng

Chairman and CEO of Vimicro International Corporation

John Deng
Source: Luyang Jiang

The Chinese government keeps in touch with illustrious expatriates, and John Deng, the first student in UC Berkeley's history to gain Master's degrees in physics and economics, and a Ph.D. in electrical engineering, was one of the most illustrious. That was why he was invited to attend the PRC's 50th anniversary ceremony in Tian'anmen Square in 1999. "I almost cried," he recalled. "It made me so proud of China. I wanted to come back and be part of it."

With the help of a government subsidy for attracting back expats, he and three friends set up Vimicro in 1999. In Deng's study, where the walls are lined with awards and honors, there is a picture of the four founders at the Great Wall.

Deng is in charge of the "China Starlight Chip Project," which has developed China's first successful integrated circuit (IC), the Starlight Multimedia IC series. On November 15, 2005, Vimicro (VIMC) became China's first NASDAQ-listed semiconductor company, and it is the largest multimedia semiconductor technology company in China.

"I'm the chairman and CEO," he said, explaining his role. "But I am also the company's spokesperson, which involves a combination of marketing, PR, and sales." At the beginning he was very "hands on" and involved in every area, even designing the company's business card and office interiors.

Like their peers in Silicon Valley, key staff at Vimicro have stock options. "People are the most important assets for a company like ours," Deng explains. "Stock options were already common in Silicon Valley start-ups, but to Chinese companies, especially in 1999, it was very advanced. But I believed it was right after seeing how it worked in Silicon Valley." Many of Vimicro's earliest hires remain with the company today.

The overseas returnees have mixed well with local talent hired from top schools, such as Tsinghua and Beijing universities, both of which are in the Zhong Guan Cun district, known as the "Silicon Valley of China." The overseas returnees are generally more senior, and train up the local hires. There are ten or so vice-presidents running their own departments. Each submits a quarterly report that includes the top three things the department and the company have achieved, and also the top three things the department and the company have failed to achieve, or need to improve. Deng says that "leadership, isn't just about the leader. To become a good leader you must be able to find good followers." He was named Person of the Year for China's Economy in 2005, and in 2009 he became the youngest ever academician of the Chinese Academy of Engineering at the age of 41.

He was on a parade float with many medals on his chest at the PRC's 60th anniversary ceremony in 2009, and his thoughts naturally turned to how he had felt watching the same parade 10 years previously. "I really made the right decision coming back," he thought.

Luyang Jiang

China's socialist market economy to establish their credentials as true sons and daughters of China, rather than renegade representatives of an alien American culture, and to demonstrate that what they are doing is consistent with the culture within which they do it.

In a ten-page article about Jack Ma (Ma Yun) in *Green Herald*, a reader who knew nothing about Ma's company, Alibaba, had to wait until page 7 for the first clues to its business. Before that the reader was informed that, not for the first time, Ma began his presentation in May 2009 at a conference in Guangzhou, dressed in traditional robes, with a display of his mastery of *Tai chi quan* (shadow boxing); that he teaches *Tai chi, jinyu* (keeping silent), and *jingzuo* (meditation) to his top executives, and believes the hardest tasks for an entrepreneur are to "rise above the self" and retain a habit of introspection while adapting to an ever-changing world.

Ma advocates a fusion of "Eastern wisdom" with "Western operation and global marketing," and has found his spiritual inspiration from Socrates, Nietzsche, and Abraham Maslow, as well Chinese sages. He seeks, in *Tai chi*, the knowledge to maintain Alibaba's "harmonious development" at a time of economic turmoil.

He told shareholders in Hong Kong in 2009 that "As the founder and CEO, I cannot cease to ask myself 'Why did I found the enterprise; what does the company exist for?'" His answer was something other than profit-making. "A company making little money is indolent and irresponsible, but companies driven purely by profit, it seems to me, are also valueless." Whether or not a company is great depends on whether it was founded on a noble ideal, and whether it creates value for the community.

Ma admires Walmart, because its founder, Sam Walton, instilled in the company the concept of "customer service." As a company grows, a seed of a dream emerges from its subconscious, which becomes a self-defining, self-driving, and self-restraining force. Alibaba's purpose is to create value for clients. Its slogan is "To make it easy to do business anywhere." The purpose emerged during the SARS epidemic in 2003, which inspired Ma to articulate three principles—change is the only unchanging thing; never place profit-making at the top of the agenda; clients come first, personnel second, and stockholders third.

He says that the wisdom of *Tai chi,* particularly the idea that in the *yin* there is *yang* and vice versa, everything consists of both, they oppose and complement each other, has allowed him to resolve a major contradiction that had confused Chinese businesspeople for 30 years: "Can enterprises adhere to their ideals, while striving to survive? Can they pursue goals loftier than profit-making while remaining profit-driven?"

Tai chi logic infuses Alibaba's management, from abstract corporate culture to the concrete behavior and performance of staff, and from abstract idealism to concrete market value and profits. There is "openness to both black and white, with equal stress on *yin* and *yang.*" The company used to have western-style "job appraisals" and set performance targets for affiliates. Now Ma merely requires top executives to reflect on what they have done at the end of each year, and assess their performance as "satisfying" or "unsatisfying."

Although among the most conspicuous, Ma is not the only philosopher showman among China's current generation of entrepreneurs. Li Shufu, founder of China's largest private auto maker, Geely, is known as the "Auto madman." He believes we live in a cosmos that is both nihilistic and eternal. He is widely regarded as among China's most successful entrepreneurs, but he says, "Within a timeframe of 10,000 years, everyone and every enterprise is a loser." Li posted his answer to the question, "What is truth?" on the wall of one of his factories in Ningbo: "A man should have basic principles in his life, without which life would be a disaster. We do proper things every day for dozens of years and we never do anything unethical."

The recent career of Liu Chuanzhi, one of China's most illustrious post-1978 entrepreneurs, illustrates some of the difficulties that can arise when the American management style confronts the Chinese culture in the same organization. Liu founded Lenovo, among China's first computer manufacturers, in 1984, but the firm only came to the attention of the west in 2005, when it bought IBM's "ThinkPad" PC business for US$1.75 billion. Following the deal Liu handed over as chairman to a Sino-American leadership team under an old IBMer initially, and then from late 2005, under a new CEO, William (Bill) Amelio, recruited from Dell.

The acquisition was not a success. According to an article in *Time* magazine in May 2010,[8] too much energy was consumed by the friction between three management tribes—the original Chinese executives, the IBM "old guard," and executives recruited by Amelio—and too little to developing new products and adapting to market trends. When Lenovo reported a $97 million loss for the three months to the end of December 2008, Liu, who had remained on the board, felt obliged to reassume control at the age of 66. "When it looked like my life['s work] was threatened, I had to come out and defend it," he said. In February 2009 his former colleague Yang Yuanqing (see above) stepped down as chairman to make room for him, and returned to the CEO job he had had before the IBM deal.

The culture clash was the main problem, in Liu's view. He felt the company had to return to its roots—to the original "Lenovo Way" (the *Dao*), a management system based on collective decision-making within a small group of senior executives. The Lenovo Way had been replaced, during the period of American leadership, by what Liu calls the "classic MBA way," where the dominant CEO makes decisions and works with business unit executives to implement them.

Liu dismisses the suggestion that the system is characteristically Chinese. "We're not following any menu," he says. Nor does he claim it is a better way than "classic MBA." He says that it is better for Lenovo, however, with its polycultural team, because "classic MBA made it difficult to mobilize or motivate teams to achieve goals."

Whatever its provenance and intrinsic merits, the Lenovo Way seems to work. The company is back in the black, thanks partly, no doubt, to the economic recovery, and is developing new products. It has reacquired a mobile phone handset maker it sold during the period of American leadership (because of the classic MBA injunction of "stick to the knitting," perhaps), and is launching ThinkPad edge, a netbook; Skylight smartbook, a cross between mini-PC and a phone; and IdeaPad Ur hybrid, a notebook with a detachable screen.

Lenovo is a special case because of its polycultural nature, but its difficulties, and how they were ultimately resolved, suggest that when management styles collide in China, the issue is likely to be resolved in favor of the indigenous Chinese culture.

Close encounter

It is, of course, inconceivable that a distinctively Chinese style of management, when it finally emerges, will be different in every respect from the allegedly "standard" American style. After three decades of until recently increasingly close association, and with so-called "sea-turtles" schooled in American management principles and techniques accounting for a significant proportion of the new generation of China's entrepreneurs, and 300 million Chinese people steeped in American culture, the imprint of American management on China's entrepreneurs is indelible.

But it is only an imprint. Many of China's successful, increasingly self-confident entrepreneurs see in the American management model not a philosophy, but merely a useful collection of techniques and operating principles, and an organizational model (the joint stock company) that provides access to international capital markets and facilitates engagement with foreign companies, and with the global economy at large.

The American model can be seen as an overlay on the older merchant tradition, which has acted as a catalyst for China's emergence as a powerful industrial economy, but which is now in the process of being retro-fitted into China's culture. The result of this retro-fit will necessarily be a hybrid of some kind, a mixture of both American and Chinese. Or, as Jack Ma suggested, a blend of eastern wisdom with western operational practices and global marketing.

It is possible, perhaps probable, that the hybrid will display the quality known, in genetics, as "hybrid vigor" or "heterosis"—the emergence, from a combination of the genetic endowments of its two parents, of a genetically superior individual, or in this case, a functionally superior management style for China.

Summary

- Entrepreneurs rather than merchants first appeared in China at the end of the nineteenth century.
- Chinese entrepreneurs believe they are strengthening China.
- There is concern that China's "entrepreneur drive" may be weakening.
- Chinese businesses consist of state-owned enterprises and three kinds of private-sector enterprise.
- The management styles of many Chinese entrepreneurs contain a strong spiritual component.

Notes

1 Smith, A. (1776) *An Inquiry into the Nature and Causes of the Wealth of Nations*, London: Ward, Lock.
2 Weber, M. (1930) *The Protestant Ethic and the Spirit of Capitalism*, London: Allen & Unwin.
3 Fu Guoyong (2009) "Seeking lost traditions of Chinese entrepreneurs," *China Entrepreneur*, September 5.
4 Kirzner, I. M. (1980) "The primacy of entrepreneurial discovery," in *Prime Mover of Progress*, Institute of Economic Affairs, IEA Readings 23.
5 Logan, D. (1990) "Tom Peters' agenda for business success," *Orange Coast Magazine*, June.
6 Qin Shou (2009) "An exploration of the drive of Chinese entrepreneurs," *Modern Management Science*, May.
7 Tawney, R. H. (1926) *Religion and the Rise of Capitalism*, John Murray.
8 Schuman, M. (2010) "Lenovo's legend returns," *Time*, May 10.

PART III

Crossing the river

CHAPTER 7

Chinese management

How can something inchoate, unformed, and as yet unacknowledged be described? The Chinese style of management is all of these things. It is still in the fetal stage, and will continue to develop, as it adapts to new situations and is exposed to new experiences. But it is already distinctive, and some of its distinctive qualities are becoming visible. So what are the qualities that will set the emerging Chinese style of management apart from other management styles?

The first point to note is that the heredity of the style has been supplied by the parents discussed in the previous three chapters. China's culture, history, and values have contributed a spiritual component. The Chinese government provides the environment, or the "land." China's entrepreneurs and merchants have contributed the energy. Spirit, land, energy. Each is powerful in its own right. Together, they create a robust and stable foundation in which each element supports the other two.

If you dig down deeply enough for an explanation for some puzzling aspect or quality of the Chinese management style you are likely to encounter eventually this triangle of forces. It is the bedrock and the source. Other things may adapt in response to circumstances or influences, but the tripod of spirit, land, and energy is immutable and immovable.

The second point to note is that this new Chinese management style both reflects and generates a distinctive management model, which incorporates western tools and methods that have proved useful for managing large companies, but is animated by and is the instrument of the Chinese management style.

On the face of it, the model is not dissimilar to the European and US management models, and many western tools and concepts, such as the Walmart, Dell, and McDonald's business models admired by Yuan Yafei, "dictator" of the HTSB group (see page 101), exert influence on or have become embedded in the Chinese way of doing business. By the similarity of shape disguises a difference in essence, just as the similarity of the whale's shape with that of fishes disguises its mammalian essence.

Nine qualities

The management style that is emerging from this triangle of forces is like a picture you can see, but cannot yet paint. It will become clearer as time passes, but in the meantime a sketch or impression of the style can be deduced from nine qualities that are likely to distinguish it from other management styles. Let us look at each of them in turn.

Dynamic

Chinese managers see their environment as being in a state of more or less permanent flux; as constantly moving and evolving. This is partly because of the central role that movement, rather than structure or shape, plays in the Chinese world view (thanks to the influence of the *I Ching*—see Chapter 4), and partly because the environment for business in China actually is more fluid and turbulent than it is in America, for example.

China's industries are, for the most part, in the relatively early stages of their evolution. There is still plenty of jockeying for position going on; still a lot of opportunities and empty niches; still a lot of growth potential, particularly in China itself. The gradual dismantling of the state sector (see Chapter 5) also gives to the business environment additional turbulence and volatility.

As most Chinese managers see it, therefore, the challenge is not to achieve a state of equilibrium adaptation to a stable competitive environment—as advocated by Michael Porter, for example—but to keep their balance in a business world where equilibrium is such a remote and distant prospect that it would be futile and foolish to try to adapt to it. The surfer shapes the wave, to some extent, of course, but for each individual surfer the wave is a given and the only imperative is to keep your balance.

Instead of devising grand strategic plans and implementing them in a deliberate and systematic way, the Chinese manager is constantly tuning and shifting distributions of weight and emphasis to try to ensure he or she does not fall off the surfboard. The rules of the business game, derived from long-established social rules, such as Confucian *li* (ritual, see Chapter 4), remain the same, but have to be applied to circumstances that are constantly changing.

Chinese managers usually have a sense of direction, but it is more like the surfer's than the military strategist's; more like a wish to reach the beach while still standing, than to arrive at a well-defined point. The mistiness of the entrepreneur's vision, combined with the turbulence and unpredictability of the environment, leads to a characteristic pattern of activity that can be summarized as periods of relatively frenetic movement interspersed by periods of relative calm. Chinese managers value both action and patience. It is a watchful patience, however; an aggressive patience disguising a readiness to act swiftly when action becomes necessary.

Adapted

Although there is no equilibrium for entrepreneurs to try to adapt to in China's business environment, there are rhythms, cycles, and seasons. Chinese managers feel the rhythms and know that there is a season for every fruit and a time for every purpose. Decisions and actions are necessary when they are necessary. The fruit will fall when it is ripe, and not before. The farmer harvests the rice when it is ready.

The government contributes its own rhythms to the environment. The People's Republic of China's (PRC's) five-year plans running from mid-decade (January 2006) to end decade (December 2010), consisting of targets in such areas as GDP, education, housing, and carbon dioxide emissions, provide Chinese businesses with a strategic background, with which their own plans need to be aligned.

In contrast to the Judaeo-Christian belief that God made the world for man, or its modern equivalent that the US government built the roads for General Motors, Chinese managers see themselves as parts of the environment, alongside whales, giant pandas, the people, and state-owned enterprises. Nothing has been created for them, and if they are to create value for themselves, they must align their own rhythms and activities with those of the environment.

The seasons and cycles cannot be hurried, or slowed down, but they can be predicted in a general sense. Summer will follow spring, and fruit will ripen in the autumn. This puts a premium on timing. The Chinese manager is always at pains to ensure that things are ready for when the seasons turn and the cycles change direction.

Flexible

If you need to keep your balance, in a turbulent and unpredictable world, you cannot afford to get too set in your ways or too wedded to a plan. Chinese managers can be precise and detailed (often for rhetorical, rather than analytical purposes) when they need to be, and they generally set great store by the "scientific method." But they also take short cuts, and value the flexibility provided by imprecision. If you have no clear plan, you have no "face" to lose if you change direction. To announce a strategy, on the other hand—and there is no point in having one if you do not announce it—is to become a hostage to fortune. If it fails, your reputation is tarnished, even if the company continues to do well.

Chinese managers are not, for example, fans of organization charts, and tend to juggle with several opportunities at once. This multitasking and parallel processing can give the western visitor the impression that there is "stop" and "go," but no focus; that in the place where you would find a clear and carefully crafted strategy in an occidental company, there is an incomprehensible fuzziness.

The western observer might acknowledge that many Chinese companies are tactically skilful, have a deep understanding of the cultural nuances of their markets, and respond quickly and appropriately to local trends. But they will insist that misty visions pursued with fuzzy logic are no substitutes for bold, clear-sighted, and well-executed strategies. Strategy plays a central role in the western management model, and Chinese companies cannot be expected, it is argued, to be competitive on the world stage, while they remain so strategically delinquent.

But suppose, for a moment, that the Chinese style is not, as it is characterized in the West, an immature and strategically deficient version of the standard western style, but is rather a new style of management based on vision and tactics, in which strategy plays a subordinate part (see page 139). As was suggested in Chapter 3 this was Deng Xiaoping's approach in 1978. He was a theatrical director with a misty vision of what he wanted China to become, content to let the "ensemble," represented in this case by spirit, land, and energy, find its way by trial and error, within certain constraints, towards the vision.

When US President John F. Kennedy launched the Apollo program on May 25, 1961, he said, "I believe that this nation should commit itself to achieving the goal, before this decade is out, of landing a man on the Moon and returning him safely to the Earth." Kennedy had little appreciation of the technical difficulties, but his vision created a reality. A few months later a janitor working at a National Aeronautics and Space Administration (NASA) facility was asked to describe his job. He said, "I am working to put a man on the moon."

When the CEO of a Chinese company, busy on tactical matters, shrugs when asked about the company's strategy, and talks vaguely about an overall vision and various possibilities and opportunities, they might be hinting at what amounts to a radically new way to run a company in the twenty-first century. Instead of a strategy the CEO has in mind a fuzzy space where balls of different colors, representing possibilities and potential opportunities and threats, are bobbing randomly about. The next step the company takes, which might in retrospect seem to have been part of a strategic sequence, will depend on which ball falls to ground first. This, in turn, will depend on what happens; what events or developments, external and internal, intrude on the fuzzy space of possibility and knock a particular ball to ground. The company's development proceeds by a series of small steps, each of which opens up a new set of adjacent possibilities.

A vision of some kind is necessary to steer the company in roughly the right direction, because as the Roman Stoic philosopher Seneca put it, "If you do not know to which port you are sailing, no wind is favorable." But because anything can happen at sea, the course you steer is always provisional.

Chinese company leaders watch and listen intently to what is going on around them, because alertness and constant scanning for weak signals that presage potential opportunities or threats are vital. What are your competitors doing? What disruptive new technologies are about to appear? What new appetites or fashions are developing among domestic and foreign consumers? What is the government going to do? How are government priorities changing; what new intentions can be read between the lines of speeches at the National People's Congress and articles in the state-owned media?

It is clear that both the occidental and Chinese approaches to the challenge of management work, in the sense that both have produced large and successful global businesses. The interesting question is, "Which approach, the strategy-driven US and European approach, or the vision-led, tactically intense Chinese approach, will prove better suited to the business conditions of tomorrow?" The short answer to this question is that it is impossible to say at this stage, but some argue that in turbulent and unpredictable environments a strategy can become a liability, because it reduces the organization's ability to adapt to changing circumstances.

A strategy is based on a linear view of the world, and assumes that there is one unique effect for each cause. In a nonlinear world a cause can have many effects. A linear system can be understood and controlled, by understanding and controlling its subsystems, but a nonlinear system behaves in a way that cannot be understood and controlled by understanding and controlling its subsystems.

Most American/European managers will acknowledge that the business environment displays some nonlinearity, but believe that this can be accommodated by adding "noise" variables to their strategies. They assume that large shocks have large effects on the system, but that the infinity of small shocks they cannot see, let alone measure, can be ignored.

Complexity scientists disagree. They say that nonlinear feedback systems, or "complex adaptive systems" as they are known, are very sensitive to initial conditions, and that small shocks can lead to dramatic changes in the behavior of the entire system. The usual example is the so-called "butterfly effect"—when taking wing in Tokyo, a butterfly can cause a gale in New York and no one will be able to trace the intervening sequence of causes and effects.

A better example nowadays is that a decision by a young home-owner in Cleveland, Ohio, to spend his limited funds on a ticket for the ballgame instead of on his mortgage repayment, brought the world's financial system to the brink of collapse via a sequence of events no one could have predicted. Or one could say that a secret agreement between 18 farmers in Xiaogang village, signed with thumbprints in November 1978, to divide land into illegal household plots led through a sequence of events no one could have predicted not only to the transformation of Chinese agriculture, but also, because of the surpluses the transformation generated, to the emergence of China as a major economic power.

If companies are also complex adaptive systems, making their way in an increasingly turbulent business environment, they cannot be guided successfully by strategies. Because it takes time for small changes to upset the system's equilibrium, tactics for managing in the short term are necessary, and scenario planning may be useful. But short-term plans may go awry, and there can be no guarantee that any scenario examined will be realized.

According to the "linear" view of business, exemplified by Michael Porter's "five forces,"[1] successful companies are those that achieve equilibrium adaptation to stable environments. Complexity science tells us that complex adaptive systems are in a state of constant disequilibrium, and are not, therefore, constrained by the environment. They co-evolve with it. This challenges a long tradition in occidental management thinking that firms can, and should seek to, achieve adaptation to a stable or slowly changing environment.

Perhaps the business environment was always unstable—perhaps the successes of the companies praised for their imaginative and well-executed strategies were fortuitous and unpredictable consequences of sequences of tactical responses to environmental stimuli, which were only construed as strategies in retrospect. In any event, it is undeniable that the business environment is less stable than it was, and it is, therefore, very possible that the Chinese style of business management, with its emphasis on vision and tactics, is better adapted to today's environment than the western style, with its emphasis on strategy.

Whether such a strategy-free Chinese style of management is suited to, or would work with, occidental companies is another question. A particular management style emerges from a particular culture. The Chinese culture, with its emphasis on harmony, mutual benefits, and optimizing in multiple dimensions, provides the constraints within which the interplays of vision and tactics drive Chinese companies forward.

There are similarities as well as differences between the American and Chinese business cultures, of course. Entrepreneurs play a key role in both, for example. But the role of the state is different (laissez-faire and reactive in the United States; centralized and proactive in China), and agency in business is also different (individuals in the United States; groups and communities of stakeholders in China). But whether or not the Chinese style of management suits them and their cultures, US and European companies may have cause to regret their addiction to strategy.

The problem with strategies is that they are relatively inflexible plans for wholly unknowable futures. They are attempts to stabilize organizations (and thus make them less agile, flexible, alert, and creative), by aligning employees with a view of the future that is certain to prove inaccurate.

For a discussion of the relationships between vision, strategy, and tactics in China, see page 139.

Foreign companies operating, or planning to operate, in China will have to resist the temptation to draw up five-year strategies with their milestones, check-points, and carefully planned sequences of tactical initiatives, and learn to watch and listen patiently, and be ready to move quickly when opportunities present themselves. It may take a while for that ball to fall from its suspension in the fuzzy cloud of potential and possibility. In the meantime, you can take a rest, while always remaining alert and watchful.

Synthetic

The Chinese management style is synthetic in the sense that it has absorbed and adapted to, and will continue to absorb and adapt to, principles, features, tools, and techniques from other management styles and traditions. There is no "not invented here" syndrome in China, as there has been in America, where new management concepts and ideas are seldom taken seriously unless they have emerged from American business schools. Chinese managers share Deng Xiaoping's view that if the cat can catch mice, its color and provenance are immaterial.

Box 7.1 Vision, strategy, tactics

The success or failure of a company depends, ultimately, on what its employees do or do not do. Action or inaction is what changes the fate of an organization for better or for worse. What a company does or does not do is in turn determined by the intention that precedes the action.

What should inspire an intention to act, a change in the environment or a plan? The conventional view is that intentions to act should be guided by a hierarchy of plans; a "vision" expressed mostly in words from which is derived a "strategy" expressed mostly in numbers, and "tactics," which although constrained by and aligned with the vision and strategy, are also inspired by the need to respond appropriately to changes in the environment.

In the West the focus of management attention is the strategy, which effectively insulates the organization from its external environment and makes tactics its servant. This strategy-led approach works well in the relatively stable environment envisaged by Michael Porter and other western strategy gurus, but becomes less effective in the less stable Chinese environment.

But although unstable, there is rhythm of a kind in China's business environment. Another reason that Chinese entrepreneurs tend to focus on vision and tactics, and regard strategy as no more than a notional link between them, is that strategy is built into their environments by the "five-year plans" of the government and the central state-owned enterprises (SOEs). The strategizing is done for them. It is part of the environment to which tactics must react appropriately.

The value of strategy, therefore, is related to the stability of the environment. The less stable the environment, the less valuable the strategy. Many large, western companies realized this in a turbulent few months between September 2008 and April 2009. Fallout from the global financial crisis had created such uncertainty, they felt they had to switch their budgeting from an annual onto a quarterly or even a monthly basis. The slow-flowing rivers they were used to crossing on clearly visible strategic stepping-stones were suddenly raging torrents. They had to cross the river, by feeling the stones.

For a while, they experienced what it is like all the time in China.

To date the American management tradition has, of course, been the most influential import, borne across the Pacific by the returning sea-turtles through the port of economic liberalism opened by Deng in 1978. But the Japanese management tradition, despite being harder for the Chinese to digest for political reasons, has also been influential and might, in other circumstances, have been the model chosen by Deng as his guide.

It is easy to exaggerate the contribution of the American style to the emerging Chinese management style, however. The fact that you hear American b-school jargon and sound-bytes, including endless references to "strategy," all the time in Chinese business circles should not be taken as evidence of the depth of American influence on Chinese business thinking. It is part of the baggage that came with the English language, and a consequence of a phenomenon well known in the West, that you get what you ask for. When westerners schooled in the strategy-led management model ask Chinese business leaders about their "strategies," they will get full western-style answers. They should not assume, however, that Chinese entrepreneurs are as committed to or focused on their "strategies" as their American counterparts would be.

It was economic liberalism, not American management thinking, that ignited China's growth explosion. American management thinking was influential, but it is becoming less so. This is partly because of the damage inflicted on the reputation of American management (and particularly its emphasis on financial engineering) by the 2007–08 global crisis, partly because Chinese entrepreneurs are more self-confident and less willing to follow, and partly because there are too many examples of uncritical applications of American ideas by Chinese companies foundering on the "spirit, land, energy" bedrock and turning out badly. The shift at the Lenovo computer group from a Chinese, to a western, and then back again to a Chinese style of management, is a case in point (see Chapter 6).

At the end of the first decade of the twenty-first century the attitude of China's entrepreneurs to foreign management ideas, techniques, and tools seems to be that they are interesting, because they have been tested in their environments of origin. They could be useful, but they will always have to be modified and adapted to the Chinese environment. The Chinese love tinkering with and adapting ideas in

Box 7.2 Zong Qinghou

Chairman and CEO of Wahaha

Zong Qinghou with the author
Photo: Luyang Jiang.

We agreed not to talk about the Danone affair when we arranged the interview with Zong Qinghou, chairman and CEO of Wahaha, China's leading water and soft drinks group. We talked about his daughter; about how she had been educated at a US business school, and come back full of ambition and eager to apply what she had learned to a Wahaha subsidiary her father had assigned to her care. He left her to it. He felt the best way to help her grow up was to let her do whatever she wanted, and to learn from her experience. "She had to feel the pain. She was too westernized," he said, shaking his head sadly. "She had to learn to listen to the local guys, and adapt to the local culture."

In his view, American managers are single-minded and treat workers as machines. Chinese workers are easier to manage, because they are more hard-working, but harder to manage too, because they think and are more flexible. "You must respect them," he says, "but you must restrict them too, by imposing constraints." He admires Mao Zedong and agrees with him that power must be centralized. Pay at Wahaha is related to performance, but everyone has an ownership stake in the company. Performance assessment is an essential part of Zong's management approach, but he says that "employees also have the right to judge their boss's performance."

Zong's old-world courtesy was surprising, in a man so demonized in the media during the Danone affair. He had two female assistants with him when we met, but when our cups needed refilling, it was Zong who got up to get the tea and hot water. His love for and his interest in his sea-turtle daughter also revealed a softer side to the Wahaha autocrat. He sees an enormous gap between his and his daughter's generations, and believes that if you want your daughter or son to listen to your suggestion, "you should show your ability first."

Whether or not it is she who succeeds him, Zong knows that he must prepare for succession. He started late as an entrepreneur, at the age of 42. He is now in his mid-60s. He sees managing succession as consisting of three tasks: create a very strong culture, formalize the rules, and establish the credibility of the successor.

But he sees plenty to do before then; from restructuring Wahaha's distribution network, to diversifying into powered milk and health products and even investing in mining in the Philippines. He has only just started planning joint ventures overseas, however. "Why go abroad with foreign partners when you have such a good home market? It would go against the rule of finishing easy tasks first and then tackling the difficult ones if we go abroad without developing the home market well," he says. Zong knows China. "Foreign companies use market research firms," he says, "but that doesn't work. We send our people out to the small cities to make notes on what's on the shelves. They speak the same language. Western companies are full of systems, but they miss the biggest picture; who the customer is."

Luyang Jiang and the author

this way. Witness the suggestion by aigo's founder, Feng Jun, that western chess could be modified by adding a sixth major piece; the Chinese cannon (see page114).

Mutual

Feng Jun's first nickname in the Chinese PC industry he has since come to dominate with his aigo brand was "five yuan Feng," after he established a strong position in the computer keyboard market by cutting his profit margin from the industry standard 50 yuan to 5 yuan. He now prefers to be known as "six wins Feng" to reflect a second mold-breaking initiative in corporate management.

His idea in 1998, after the market for his Little Sun products had been invaded by a plague of fakes, was to set out the basis of the relationships between his company, Huaqi, and what might be called in the West its "stakeholders." Henceforth, Feng announced, Huaqi would be run in a way that reconciled the reasonable interests and development opportunities of six constituencies: the "public," by which he meant existing and prospective customers, "agencies" (the company's distributors), employees, the company itself, suppliers, and society at large. It was a shift from "win over" to "win with."

Although new to the Chinese computer industry, which had inherited its business model from its American progenitor, the idea that the company was part of a group of constituencies that depended on one another, and had a mutual interest in, and claims on value created in the positive sum game of business, is entirely in tune with the emphasis placed in Chinese culture on reciprocal obligations. The inclusion of society in Feng's six interested parties also echoes the belief of China's early nineteenth-century entrepreneurs (see Chapter 6) that they were contributing to the strength of China.

The cultural origins of Feng's "six wins" are also reflected in the importance many Chinese managers attach to the intangible outcomes from their business activities, such as trust, employee, customer and supplier loyalty, and generally good relationships with all of the company's interested parties. This, in turn, is reflected in typically complex and multi-faceted performance measurement models that make the "balanced scorecard," developed by Robert Kaplan and David Norton, look simple by comparison.

When Jack Ma abandoned western-style "job appraisals," and instead asked his executives whether their performance was "satisfying" or "unsatisfying" (see Chapter 6), he was not simplifying performance assessment. He was shifting from a complicated, external appraisal system to a much more complicated self-assessment system.

Another manifestation of the cultural importance of reciprocity or mutual obligation in China is the approach of Chinese companies to human resources management. Many Chinese entrepreneurs dislike the term "HR," because they do not see their people as resources. They prefer the older English term "personnel."

Employees are members of the corporate family. While they help the company to achieve success, which is also their success, they have a right to expect opportunities to grow and develop as people, and realize their potential. It can be summarized as the three "Ls":

- Legacy: Being part of a successful company moving to a realization of the leader's vision that will survive you.
- Learning: Self-fulfillment and realization of potential.
- Life/love: Family atmosphere involving care for members.

This contrast with what might be called the cash and career-driven western model reflects the fascination of the Chinese with dynasty, and what each emperor/entrepreneur bequeaths to those who follow. The employees work for the benefit of "the boss," who rewards and cares for them in return. "Everyone needs to feel 'included' in the organization", Yuan Yafei explained (see page 101). HR appraisal systems are informal, like Jack Ma's satisfaction self-assessment, rather than based on the formal, highly analytical key performance indicators favored at US companies.

This is a world away from "Management by objectives" and Frederick Taylor's "scientific management." Although not unknown in the West, this idea that business consists of indefinitely long series of encounters with several classes of interested parties, and that winning one encounter, by aggressive negotiation, for example, or other practices indicating the belief that "nice guys finish last," will compromise or possibly preclude subsequent encounters, never really took root.

It crops up from time to time in the now largely forgotten idea of employee "empowerment," and in "customer relationship management," although the latter was associated more with systems and software than with a philosophy. Lip service is paid to the ideas of mutual interests and reciprocal obligation, but unlike their counterparts in China, western managers seldom act as if they believe in them.

Consensual

If you look at the distributions of power in China through western eyes you see tyranny everywhere, from the all-powerful Chinese Communist Party (CCP) and its local "party bosses" in government and the all-powerful patriarchs in families, to the all-powerful CEO bosses in companies. In terms of the structure of Chinese society and of its social institutions the perception is accurate. It is misleading for western observers, however, because it obscures the differences in the occidental and oriental meanings of the word "boss."

The authority of the "boss" in western cultures stems from what the person achieved to reach the position. Although the same kinds of qualities and achievement are required to reach a boss position in China, once reached, the authority of the boss comes not from what the boss did to become boss, but from the boss position itself.

Three millennia of dynastic rule in China have instilled the shape of a hierarchy in the national psyche, presided over by an emperor or "key leader," as Guo Zhenxi puts it (see page 58). The "boss" is integral to the well-ordered Confucian society, but—and this is the crucial point—it brings with it obligations. The mandate to rule (the Mandate of Heaven, see Chapter 4) is conditional on the ruler's good behavior. "The people" acknowledge the need for a ruler to guide them and make decisions when decisions have to be made, but reserve the right to oppose and, if necessary, to depose a bad ruler.

The condition attached to a mandate to rule, and the motivation of rulers to ensure people do not invoke it, have two consequences for the emerging Chinese management style.

The first is that good leaders acknowledge as legitimate claims of employees on the value they help to create. The unwritten contract of employment is that if you work hard to enrich your bosses, they will give you something back. This bargain was reflected in the preference Chinese companies displayed during the aftermath of the financial crisis for across-the-board salary cuts. The alternative of headcount reductions would have seemed like eating the family.

The second consequence of the conditional mandate is that although bosses make the decisions in what appears to be a classic "top-down" manner, they will only do so after long and exhaustive discussions with advisers. Once again, it is the emperor model: the boss consults widely with counselors representing the opinions of all the people to ensure the decisions reached are acceptable. The "Lenovo way" (see Chapter 6) exemplifies the system.

As we have seen in Chapter 5, this search by the ruler for a broad consensus is also evident in the way China is governed. Decisions to shift the emphasis or directions of policy are only taken after lengthy discussions and debates of "leaked" proposals. This is why communications, with close colleagues in companies, and with party factions and circles, academics and think-tanks in government, are so important in China.

The need to reach a broad consensus that goes beyond acceptance or "buy-in" suggests that, if management styles can be characterized by their preferred applications media, the Chinese style favors Microsoft Word documents, because its objectives are to persuade and seek feedback, while the American style favors PowerPoint, because its objectives are to explain and instruct.

Spiritual

It would strike employees of a western company as odd if their CEO invoked a higher spiritual power to explain the company's purpose, or win their commitment to a new strategy. Shareholders might also be uneasy if it became apparent that the agent they had appointed to further their interests owed allegiance to another being, or was committed to a purpose other than shareholder value maximization.

It is not that westerners are less religious than the Chinese. The evidence indicates the opposite (see Chapter 4). It is that in the West, business operates in a material world separate from the world of the spirit, and is driven by a material purpose about which the spiritual world has nothing to say.

In China, the spiritual and material are aspects of the same world, and it would be odd if a CEO did not use the power of the spiritual principles and concepts embedded in China's culture and languages, to communicate with the company's various "stakeholders," and seek the commitment of employees to realizing the CEO's vision. One of the key qualities that distinguishes successful, from unsuccessful Chinese entrepreneurs is the skill and sensitivity with which they deploy the powerful communications medium provided by the cultural and spiritual heritage shared by all China's people.

The best Chinese business leaders communicate with their employees at a spiritual as well as a material level. When Li Dongsheng, CEO of TCL Corporation, embarked on a reconstruction of TCL's culture in 2006, he called the project "Rebirth of the Eagle" (see Chapter 6). The eagle is an evocative symbol, full of cultural meaning in China. Where a western CEO would use tools, frameworks, and PowerPoint presentations to convince employees of the need for change, Chinese leaders would use value-laden metaphors, myths, and legends from Chinese culture. They are story tellers and dream weavers.

A company adapted to the Chinese environment and to the trinity of spirit, land, and energy, is, by definition, a spiritual as well as a material institution. This is why tools and techniques imported from another management style sometimes lead to outcomes that are the opposite of what was intended, because they are rejected by the firm's spiritual immune system.

Disciplined

Although fuzzy in its logic and spiritual in its communication, the emerging Chinese management style is not "pink and fluffy," as they say in the United States. The leadership system at SOEs and the large private-sector companies is modeled on the system of government; the CEO (emperor/premier) and an inner circle of close advisers (Politburo Standing Committee) supported by a powerful, well-staffed *dong ban* (chairman's office—see Chapter 8), which includes a discipline department. The personnel performance review cycle is short, often monthly. Staff training is extensive and regimented, much like the training at the Central Party School (see Chapter 5).

The importance that private-sector Chinese business leaders attach to discipline and regimentation is indicated by the fact that the People's Liberation Army (PLA) is a source of inspiration for some of them. It is very clear in Chinese companies that betraying "the boss" is a firing offence.

Suning, China's largest consumer durable retailer, is organized on CCP lines. The chairman deals with the provincial level and above, and the CEO deals with the lower levels and the operational people doing the work. There is a strong if somewhat disorganized culture of discipline.

Natural

All management styles are "natural," in the sense that they emerge and are not deliberately or consciously designed. But they emerge in particular places and at particular times. The management style that Chinese entrepreneurs, particularly the sea-turtles, adopted during the 30-year American experiment emerged in mid-nineteenth-century America. At that time, and in that place it was "natural," and can be said to have been invoked by its environment.

But early twenty-first century China is very different from mid-nineteenth-century America, and if the slate of history could be wiped clean it seems unlikely that China today would invoke a management style the same as or even similar to the American style. The slate cannot be wiped clean—the Chinese management style will be forever marked by its youthful adoption of the American style—but it can be adapted to its new environment so completely that the original American model becomes almost invisible.

That is what is happening now. The Chinese management style is being "naturalized": growing closer to the style that would have emerged if there had been no US model. It is becoming "natural" in another sense, too. It is emerging from the spirit, land, energy trinity, rather from a military model with its officers and strategies, and its identification of competition with war, which was the original template for the American style.

It is complicated, because it is a bridge between the rational and the emotional, the tangible and the intangible, the material and the spiritual. It is subtle, because it is sensitive to cycles and seasons, and the environment. It is fuzzy and difficult to master. To use a word much over-used in the West, it is "organic," and likely to create its own business "ecosystem," in China at any rate, and perhaps further afield.

Chinese managers

It is in the nature of an emergent phenomenon that people directly contributing to the emergence will be unaware of it. Chinese managers are not trying to invent a management style. They are simply trying to make their companies work better by tinkering a little here, changing a little there; finding their way by trial and error to a better way to manage. Few of them talk of a Chinese management style, and even fewer could say what is distinctive about it.

But when asked about it, many are interested in the idea that there could be such a thing as a Chinese management style, and that, as their companies prosper and they become more comfortable in their roles as contemporary heroes, they are contributing to it whenever they dispense with or modify some element of the American style, or add some principle or concept derived from Chinese culture. The way negatives can build, as well as destroy, is exemplified by the widespread dislike of PowerPoint in China, and of what some of the new generation of entrepreneurs regard as the "cartoon" quality of the western management style.

Discussions with Chinese entrepreneurs about management style will often end up at the spirit, land, energy trinity. They cherish the past and the 3,000 years of cultural development, because it gives a context for their own achievements. Most of them approve of the Chinese government, because it gives them a sense of direction and they trust it. The see themselves, and their fellow entrepreneurs, as contributing to China's growing economic might, and as cultured realists with no time for the "cartoon" management exemplified by PowerPoint. They talk endlessly about "strategy," in the American B-school idiom, but usually the gist of it all is that they have a vision and they are crossing the river by feeling the stones.

Some have done OK using an unadulterated American management style at their companies. Others have not. "For the first five years I applied, by the book, ideas and concepts I had learned at Harvard Business School," said a second-generation entrepreneur from Hong Kong operating in real estate and manufacturing in mainland China. "I was the worst manager my company has ever had. Since then I have followed my cultural instincts first, and have been extremely successful. That meant adapting the HBS concepts and framework."

Some have tried to get what they see as the best of both worlds by being "Chinese on the outside, American on the inside." The risk with such a policy is that you appear inconsistent or hypocritical to insiders and outsiders. It is true that the Chinese management style will be a hybrid (see Chapter 5), but it will be a hybrid through and through, not one pure breed on the inside, and another on the outside.

The general impression Chinese entrepreneurs convey to an outsider is that they are between two worlds. Their talk of China's culture and the world of the spirit is not, as they think some outsiders believe, mere marketing. They believe in it and take it seriously. They are reaching back for Chinese culture, and have only just begun to incorporate its principles and teaching in the ways they manage their businesses. It is such a slow process that it is invisible to most of them, but as suggested at the beginning of the chapter, the fetus of a genuinely Chinese management style shows every sign of being viable.

Many Chinese entrepreneur CEOs see themselves as reincarnations of the Industrial Revolution entrepreneurs of the eighteenth century, or the American tycoons of the late nineteenth century. There are similarities, to be sure, but the spirit, land, energy trinity is so strong, and differentiates modern China so significantly from the environments of their western antecedents, that the comparison is misleading. They are citizens of a "civilization state," as Martin Jacques put it,[2] not of a nation state, and they, their management styles, and their companies will bear the imprint of their civilization.

Organization

Like management styles, business forms emerge in particular places at particular times. The "environment of evolutionary adaptedness" (EEA), as evolutionists call it, of the business form that Chinese entrepreneurs adopted after Deng Xiaoping's opening up in 1978 was also mid-nineteenth-century America. Alfred Chandler, its most eminent historian, called it the multi-unit business enterprise (MuBE) and explained its emergence with eight propositions.[3]

His first proposition was that the MuBE replaced small traditional enterprises when "routinizing" business transactions reduced their costs, linking together the administration of production, buying, and distribution reducing information costs, and internalizing many units allowed the "administrative co-ordination" of flows of goods between units, leading to better scheduling, more intensive use of resources (including people), higher productivity, lower costs, and more certain cash flow.

Chandler believed savings from administrative coordination, which he said was "the central function of modern business enterprise," were much greater than information and transaction cost savings. In this he took issue with Ronald Coase, who had earlier suggested that the reason integrated organizations had evolved was that, by suppressing internal price systems, they saved the "transaction costs" that arose when markets balanced supply and demand.[4]

Coase's ideas were later developed into a broad theory of the firm by his student Oliver Williamson, who suggested that "The modern corporation is mainly to be understood as the product of a series of organizational innovations that have had the purpose and effect of economizing on transaction costs."[5]

Whether, as Chandler believed, it was the cost savings produced by administrative coordination, or as Coase and Williamson thought, it was transaction cost economies, that gave the MuBE its edge, it seems clear that advances in information technology (IT) since the MuBE's emergence have changed its EEA out of all recognition. As a consequence, life is much easier now for those small traditional enterprises the MuBE conquered in the early twentieth century, and it is likely that if the tape was run again now, the MuBE would find it much harder to beat them.

That at any rate is how Alibaba, China's leading internet services company, sees it. Its declared mission is "to make life easier for small business owners." Founder Jack Ma and his colleagues talk of a "post-industrial era" of "specialized logistics," "personalized marketing" and "flexible manufacture" that gives China a chance to overtake other countries, and lead the world into a new commercial age dominated by small and medium-sized enterprises (SMEs). "When internal management and external cooperation can be achieved more efficiently via the internet the economic mode of all society will be changed," they say. In "Green mode," as Alibaba people call this new post-industrial era, conflict and competition will be replaced by "harmony—between companies, between employers and employees, suppliers and consumers," and a new commercial culture focused less on the commerce and more on the culture will blossom.

In the West such a vision would seem implausible, because the MuBE is too dominant and well-established. In China it is more credible, because private Chinese companies are younger—most are still run by their founders—and their development paths are more open. The central SOEs will remain the backbone of the Chinese economy, but armies of SMEs are likely to be its heart, much as the *Mittelstand* are the heart of the German economy.

If China is leading the world into a new, SME-dominated era, there should be signs, in the form of differences, not only in the style of management at Chinese companies, but also in the organizational forms they take. It is still early days, but it seems possible, for instance, that mature Chinese companies will end up "thinner" than their western counterparts, in the sense that they will tend to occupy smaller segments of their value chains. It is not that they will "outsource" more than western companies; it is that the level of inter-firm coordination made possible by modern communications, particularly the internet, is so high they will not feel a need to "insource" in the first place. The "thinness," if it does become a distinctive quality of Chinese enterprises as they mature, will be an unconscious adaptation, rather than a consequence of deliberate decisions to be less vertically integrated.

Another distinctive feature Chinese companies may display as they mature is relatively low gearing. There are some signs, including the appetite many Chinese entrepreneurs have for property assets, that they feel the need for more substance in their balance sheets than western company leaders, who are taught at the B-schools about capital efficiency and the "debt control hypothesis" that sees the interest rate as the correct hurdle rate for new investment.

But this presupposes that all private Chinese companies are still immature. Perhaps they are not. Perhaps they are the next stage in the evolution of enterprise form. Natural evolution works this way in a process known as neoteny (literally "holding youth"). We are the creatures of neoteny. Our bulbous cranium, containing our large brain, resembles that of a fetal ape. Subsequent ape brain growth is slower, so the cranial vault is smaller and lower in adults. We acquired our large brains by retaining rapid fetal growth rates.

Perhaps private Chinese companies will retain to maturity features that seem to western eyes to be fetal, and thus establish a new standard corporate form. Perhaps that fetus is already viable.

Summary

- The Chinese management style is emerging from the spirit, land, energy trinity.
- It displays nine characteristics: dynamic, adapted, flexible, synthetic, mutual, consensual, spiritual, disciplined, and natural
- The value of strategy is proportional to the stability of the business environment.
- Chinese entrepreneurs are between two worlds.
- Mature Chinese companies may turn out to be "thinner" than mature western companies.

Notes

1 Porter, M. (1980) *Competitive Strategy*, New York: Free Press.
2 Jacques, M. (2009) *When China Rules the World,* London: Penguin Press.
3 Chandler, A. (1977) *The Visible Hand: The Managerial Revolution in American Business*, Cambridge, Mass.: Harvard University Press.
4 Coase, R. (1937) *The Nature of the Firm*, Economica.
5 Williamson, O. (1981) "The modern corporation: origins, evolution, attributes," *Journal of Economic Literature*, Vol. 19, No. 4, pp. 1537–68.

CHAPTER 8

Strangers in a strange land

A wise man walking from one town to another met a stranger walking the other way. "You won't like the people in that town," said the stranger turning and pointing the way he had come. "They're unfriendly, devious and secretive. What are people like in the town you have come from?"

"I expect you will find they're much the same," said the wise man.

Later in the day, the wise man met another stranger walking in the other direction. "You will like the people in that town," said the stranger pointing the way he had come from. "They are friendly, straightforward and honest. What are people like in the town you have come from?"

"I expect you will find they're much the same," said the wise man.

How western firms operating in China already, planning to enter it, or dealing in any way—as partners, collaborators, customers, or suppliers—with Chinese businesses or business people (and in the medium to long term that includes practically every western firm) perceive the country and its people, will depend more on them than on China. It is the set you have to the country that will determine whether or not you prosper in China.

The wise man will acknowledge, however, that towns can change, and the allegation of some westerners is that China has withdrawn the welcome mat laid down for foreign companies in 2001 at the time of China's accession to the World Trade Organization (WTO).

Understanding the environment

Perhaps the clearest sign that China's attitude to foreigners, and their business resources, has been changing in recent years is the Enterprise Income Tax Law, effective from January 1, 2008.

China's previous corporate income tax (CIT) system was designed to attract overseas capital to help finance growth. The priorities of the period were evident in the generous tax incentives for foreign investment enterprises (FIEs) in which foreigners owned 25 percent or more of the shares. They included reinvestment relief, which gave refunds (normally 40 percent of taxes paid) to foreign investors that reinvested their shares of FIE profits; reduced CIT rates for FIEs of 15 percent in special economic zones (less than half the standard CIT rate of 33 percent) and 24 percent in open coastal economic zones; a two-year tax holiday, followed by a 50 percent rate reduction to production enterprises operating for at least ten years, and complete exemption from the dividend withholding tax.

The new CIT law replaced the dual system, under which the taxation of FIEs was governed by this special law, and put FIEs on the same tax footing as wholly Chinese-owned companies. There were transitional arrangements for FIEs already enjoying incentives, but most FIE incentives, including reinvestment relief and dividend withholding tax exemption, were withdrawn.

The message was clear. China had come of age, financially. Foreign direct investment was still welcome, but no longer needed. There were reduced rates in the new law for "high-technology" businesses (defined more narrowly than previously) and for small companies of 15 percent and 20 percent respectively, but there was no distinction between foreign and domestic companies.

Other features of the new CIT law reflected China's transformation from supplicant to a fully fledged and financially self-sufficient member of the global economy. The CIT rate was cut from 33 percent to 25 percent, reflecting the global shift from direct to indirect taxation, new "thin-capitalization" rules denied deductibility of interest on related-party debt in excess of a certain ratio, a new Controlled Foreign Company rule applied to profits of enterprises established in jurisdictions where the tax rate was "significantly lower" than China's 25 percent rate, and a General Anti-Avoidance Rule, the defining characteristic of a modern, sophisticated tax regime, denied tax benefits to any transaction lacking "reasonable business objectives." These changes certainly make China's tax regime less welcoming for foreigners, but only because they remove privileges not previously shared by domestic Chinese companies.

There are other complaints by foreign firms that indicate China is developing a more self-assured, more self-sufficient, and generally more sophisticated relationship with the world economy. New government procurement rules issued in 2009 are said to favor local suppliers and "indigenous innovation." New rules for patents issued in February 2010 are said to threaten to increase costs in China for foreign innovators in the pharmaceuticals industry, and oblige them to license drug production to local firms at state-set prices. Foreign manufacturers of wind generators and solar panels say they are being excluded from large renewable-energy projects. Regulatory barriers limit foreign involvement in China's insurance market. More generally, China's government is said to be grooming state-owned enterprises (SOEs) as "national champions," at the expense of private Chinese companies as well as of foreign firms.[1]

If these complaints by foreign firms are justified it would not be surprising, or unusual in a developing country. As Li Yi, chairman and country head of UBS China, said during an interview on Phoenix TV's *Finance P2P* program, "every country would protect its national and local industries." In the 1950s and 1960s, Japan's Ministry of International Trade and Industry (MITI) promoted Japan's domestic industries, and protected them from international competition. As Japanese industry became stronger, MITI's role changed; it became involved in easing international tension created by the success of Japan's exporters by, for example, organizing voluntary restraints on automobile exports to the United States.

The wise man would understand these stages of economic development that the towns he was walking between might be passing through, and yet he would still give the same answers to the travelers he met. These are the kinds of changes that foreign companies operating in or dealing with China should have expected. The real challenge for the foreign companies, according to Li Yi, is that:

> their [domestic] rivals are growing stronger. Their understanding of policies and markets poses a huge challenge to foreign enterprises … they not only know very well about their native culture, [they] are also fast learners of good management mechanisms from abroad … foreign companies should … adjust their state of mind, carefully study the market, integrate into it and join the competition.

It is becoming harder for foreign firms to prosper in China as tax and industrial policies adapt to the succeeding stages of economic development, domestic firms become stronger competitors, and a new, characteristically Chinese management style emerges, to which they must adapt. But at the same time China is becoming an ever larger, more important, and increasingly essential market for any company with global ambitions. Steering clear of, or quitting, the country because of a tougher regulatory environment, a more nationalistic industrial policy, the withdrawal of tax privileges, tougher local competitors, or new management challenges is not an option.

Know yourself

When adapting to the new Chinese management style, foreigners will find it helpful to remember the often unconscious prejudices they bring with them from their own management cultures, traditions, and styles. It is easy to over-generalize, because variations within management cultures are usually greater than variations between them, but the common perceptions of the US and European management styles can be summarized as follows.

The American style

Shareholders first

The fundamental credo of the western management styles is that the ultimate duty of managers is owed to the company's owners, and thus the ultimate objective of managers should be the maximization of shareholder value.

Too much is sometimes made of this. Shareholder value maximization is not so much an objective as a *raison d'être*. In a free market in corporate control, a publicly listed company whose managers did not endeavor to maximize shareholder value would be vulnerable to a takeover. Moreover, the shareholder maximization imperative in the American culture leaves open the question of "how" shareholder value is most effectively maximized. Only shareholders can hold managers to account, but if managers fail to take into account the interests of the non-owning "stakeholders," they will find it hard to create value for anyone.

It is also important to be clear about the meaning of "value." In a private company, or a publicly listed company in which the founder or his or her family retains effective control, "value" might mean something other than market value, such as a reputation for being a responsible corporate citizen, for looking after employees in an economic downturn, or contributing to the well-being of society at large.

In practice, however, shareholders' interests do loom larger in US management thinking than in European management thinking, and this can lead to differences in decision-making and priority-setting.

Short-termism

Associated with shareholder value maximization is a preoccupation with short-term performance, or "quarteritis," as it is known. This is said to be at the expense of obviously healthier, long-term profit-maximizing strategies. The fault here is alleged to lie with myopic capital markets that measure management performance on a quarterly basis.

Inequality

Extremely high levels of executive pay are not only tolerated, but seen as a virtue, because they motivate others. They are currently seen as very unfair, however, because the 2007–08 financial crisis has cast doubt on the competence of top executives; there is no, or at any rate very little, connection between pay and performance; and executive pay levels are contributing to growing inequality in the United States which threatens to undermine the social consensus from which the American management style derives its legitimacy.

Individualism

Incentives, usually money, are mostly focused on individual rather than team performance. A so-called "bonus culture" permeates the whole system. In some sectors, such as investment banking, bonuses are so high, even after the financial crisis, that they are being seen by many ordinary people as evidence that the entire system is fundamentally flawed.

Business as war

Partly as a consequence of very high levels of pay and bonuses for individuals, business is widely seen as a zero-sum game in which "nice guys finish last." Companies led by highly paid all-powerful CEOs "fight" aggressively for supremacy, and try to "defeat" their

Box 8.1 Zhou Hongyi

CEO of Qihoo.com, venture capitalist

Zhou Hongyi, cyber warrior
Source: Luyang Jiang

Zhou Hongyi is a walking contradiction. On entering his office the first thing I noticed was the rifle-shooting target on one wall. That seemed to corroborate his reputation as a pugnacious internet entrepreneur developing software warriors to do battle in the virus/antivirus war zone, who always seemed to be either fighting or spoiling for a fight.

At first sight the opposite wall confirms the impression. Enormous speakers; megawatt amplifier—this guy likes loud. But one glance at Zhou's CD collection spoils the picture. Western classics by Mozart and Beethoven, Chinese pop songs from the 1980s and 1990s, movie soundtracks; how does that fit in? "Is your blood group A-B?" I asked. "How did you know?" he replied.

Later at his team-building place out of town I watched him playing laser-gun war games with colleagues, and realized he's a big kid. A smart, and very successful kid for whom twitter rows, blog battles, and law suits are just another form of combat.

Zhou sold his first company, 3721, which was backed by an American venture capital fund, to US group Yahoo in 2003, for US$120 million. He was appointed president of Yahoo China in 2004. He quit in 2005 when Yahoo China was acquired by Jack Ma's Alibaba group (see page 124), and launched Qihoo.com, a blog and bulletin board aggregator and search engine, backed by a California venture fund.

A venture capitalist himself now—he is always on the lookout for guys with good ideas, who talk his language—Zhou has experienced the American and Chinese management models from the inside. "Most international companies, especially American companies, that operate in China use the same model," he said. "The CEO in China is a figurehead and coordinator, rather than a leader. Every business department reports to the appropriate department at headquarters, rather than to the Chinese CEO." Zhou thinks this model could work OK with companies that sell tangible products, such as Cisco, Dell, and Microsoft, but said that "the internet industry sells service, and this needs fast updating and adaptation to consumer needs. In this business a long response chain is a competitive weakness."

He advises a service provider planning to enter the Chinese market to cooperate with a local venture team. "It can help the foreign company to localize in China. The right to make strategy decisions must always remain with the local entrepreneur."

On whether or not the emerging Chinese management model will prove superior to the American model, Zhou thinks the jury is still out. "People judge a hero by victory or defeat," he said. "The histories of most successful Chinese companies today are less than 15 years. The founders are still the key people. Few local Chinese companies hire MBA graduates to manage their companies. Their development is like 'crossing the river by feeling the stones.' It's a process of experiment. Most founders are businessmen, not entrepreneurs. It's too early to judge their success and their management model."

Luyang Jiang

competitors. This is why Sun Tzu's *The Art of War* (see Chapter 4) is so popular among the American management elite. The weaknesses of this Darwinian "red in tooth and claw" approach are that it can lead to a combative corporate culture, and inhibit the adoption of cooperative, partnership-based approaches to business which might in some circumstances create more value.

Strengths

If the above five qualities seem negative, it should be recognized that the American management style has been enormously successful on most measures, both at home and abroad. Its strengths include a rapid decision-making process, formidable capital-raising powers, high capital efficiency, and an organizational structure that makes it less dependent than the Chinese management style on the quality and survival of the leader. It has proved its ability to transfer power from one leader to another without excessive disruption, and it can operate effectively without a leader for extended periods.

The European style

The Chinese do not normally distinguish between US and European management styles. They see the latter as merely a variant of the former. This perception is broadly accurate, but there are several important differences between US and European styles, and it seems fair to say that the European style is somewhat closer to the emerging Chinese style of management than the US style.

European managers are said to focus more on the long term and take more account of non-owning stakeholders than their counterparts in the United States. They have more experience in managing cultural, linguistic, and ethnic diversity; their long history of colonialism and cross-border trade has given them a more international outlook, and their political tradition of social democracy has led to a more positive attitude within the business community towards government.

That variations within groupings can be greater than those between them is evident here; the UK management style is generally seen as closer to the US than to the continental European style.

The impression that the European management style is closer to the emerging Chinese style than the American style, at least as far as the attitude of business to the state is concerned, was confirmed by a Roland Berger survey of senior executive opinions.[2] Two-thirds of American respondents felt the state "reduces the success and growth potential of my company," against 46 percent of European respondents, and 9 percent of Chinese respondents.

Most Chinese respondents (57 percent) agreed with the comment that the government "ensures a stable business environment," against 44 percent in Europe and 34 percent in the United States, and a third of Chinese respondents agreed that the state "boosts the prospects of success and growth potential of my company," compared with only 16 percent of European respondents, and a meager 7 percent of US respondents.

Although European managers may therefore find it easier than Americans in some respects to adapt to the Chinese management style, it should not be inferred from this that, in moving away from the American style of management, Chinese managers are moving towards the European style. The emerging Chinese management style is nothing so simple as a shift in the focus of inspiration from the United States to Europe. It is coming from the spirit, land, energy bedrock. It will be Chinese. The Europeans will have as much adapting to do as the Americans.

The adaptive challenge

Foreign firms have their strengths in China, even today. They have experience in different countries, for example, and take a longer-term view than Chinese firms. But their strengths are no longer a perfect match with China's weaknesses. In the first 30 years after the opening-up in 1978, China needed everything that foreign firms brought—money, business, models, technology, and so on—and for this reason, the engagement between foreign and Chinese enterprises was relatively easy.

Now that China's relative weaknesses are no longer such a perfect match with the strengths of foreign firms, and Chinese entrepreneurs are more self-sufficient and self-confident, and less willing to take western business wisdoms for granted, the relationship has entered a new phase. China has become a stranger land for strangers, and a new form of engagement between foreign and Chinese enterprise must be found.

Foreign firms have three options. They can decide it is all getting too difficult to make money in China, and give up. They can take the view that the problem is not with the western business models, tools, and approaches themselves, but with the piecemeal way they have been "sold" in China, and try to sell them more effectively. Or they can accept that the pendulum that was previously bringing Chinese business closer and closer to the western model has begun to swing the other way, that the adaptive challenge is therefore theirs rather than China's, and try to understand what is going on and how they can contribute.

When assessing the adaptive challenge facing foreign companies and their managers in China, it is helpful to distinguish between three different categories of foreign enterprise:

Old hands

Foreign companies that have been operating in China for many years should be all right as long as they keep their ears to the ground, sense what is going on, and adapt. They know the rules of the game and are aware of the need for patience. But they should be careful not to oppose the emergence of, or refuse to engage with, the new Chinese management model by insisting that the "old" western ways are the best ways. Long-established foreign companies were the ambassadors of the American model, and had authority for that reason. They have lost that authority, and must establish themselves as contributors of value within the new model.

Recent arrivals

Firms that have been operating in China for five years or less and lack the networks and established substance of the "old hands" are more vulnerable. Their markets will be seen as targets by domestic companies, their profitability will be eroded by the withdrawal of tax incentives, and they could suffer from the Chinese government's more nationalistic industrial policies (see above). They will need to adapt quickly, if they are not to be wiped out.

Newcomers

New arrivals from abroad must recognize that they will be bringing no authority with them, and should clear their minds of prejudices and preconceptions associated with western management models. It is a new ballgame in China. There are no blueprints or charts. What might have been a competitive advantage a few years ago might now be a disadvantage. Watch carefully. Listen attentively. Don't rush. Don't assume that causes and levers have the same effects in China as in your country of origin.

Because relationships both between and within companies ultimately boil down to personal relationships, these categories get mixed up in practice.

Some companies that rank as "old hands," in terms of the time they have been operating in China, may include, or be led by people who have arrived relatively recently. This is actually quite common in China. Foreign-owned Chinese businesses experiment with different local leaders, approaches, and styles, because in China's changing business environment, approaches that worked fine a few years back may be less effective now.

This can be illustrated by the quasi-fictional tale of an "old hand" firm, which began one day in 1984 when three Chinese managers who had studied in Germany and were working for a European company were called into their boss's office and told they were fired. But there was good news too. They were asked to open an outpost of the company in Shanghai. They accepted.

It was a brave move barely six years after Deng Xiaoping's opening-up and eight years before his "southern tour." Although there was plenty of demand for the company's products in China, no conventions had been established about pricing or terms of engagement. It was frontier territory. The Chinese founders of the fledgling offshoot of the European firm had to keep their ears close to the ground, and pick up bits and pieces of business here and there, wherever and whenever opportunities presented themselves. There was some direction from Europe, but there was no blueprint for entering a market such as China, with such enormous potential, but at such an early stage of its development.

The firm did well. It had entered China so soon after the opening-up that it was almost indigenous. It grew organically, as China grew, and did well enough to encourage the European parent to convert it into a wholly owned foreign enterprise (WOFE) when that form of business became legal in 1994. The founders left when WOFE status was granted, and a European professional who had been running the firm's Tokyo office took over the leadership. A Beijing office was opened the following year. The firm prospered for a decade with a leader who understood the role expected of him in a country with a long tradition of imperial rule.

In 2004 several managers were recruited from leading US firms in the same industry. Although ethnically Chinese, most had American passports, and all were steeped in the American business culture. The scene was set for a culture clash, with the European "emperor" caring for his "family" of employees on one side, representing the traditional Chinese model, and the new "sea-turtle" recruits on the other side advocating a more professional, American approach.

The sea-turtles won, and the "emperor" was gradually edged out over three years, before the end of which time the sea-turtles had also left. The leadership position was filled by a German manager who only stayed for a year. He was replaced in late 2006 by another European. Under the watchful eye of the still-to-depart "emperor" emeritus the new leader adopted a Chinese style of management, and the firm has prospered ever since.

Although much-needed stability returned to the firm after a period of constant leadership changes, the new boss encountered unusually turbulent meteorological, geological, and financial environments in his first three years in office. In September 2007 he flew his staff and their families (about 200 people) to Jejudo, a volcanic island off the south-west coast of Korea, for the firm's annual outing. In the afternoon of September 12, a Tropical Cyclone Formation Alert was issued for a depression that would intensify rapidly over the next two days, to become the category 4 typhoon Nari (Korean for "lily"). There was an option to rush to the airport, but only 14 seats were available on the last flight out of Jejudo, before Nari was due to make landfall. None of the firm's Chinese employees and their families could take the seats, because they were on a joint visa, but there was room on the plane for the firm's senior executives, including the boss and his wife and two children.

It was a perfect career-defining dilemma for a leader who had been in office (and China) for less than a year, and was committed to a Chinese style of management. Should he fly his family to safety, or should he stay with and support his new, now endangered "corporate family"?

As is an emperor's habit, he consulted his wife and colleagues. The advice he received was typically Chinese in its equivocation: "If you go they will understand; if you stay they will appreciate it." The imperial family stayed. It was rough. The beleaguered emperor and his retinue suffered the privations of no electricity and limited food for a day, and although Nari weakened to tropical storm strength before it hit Jejudo, 20 people lost their lives in the subsequent flooding. The emperor/boss emerged from the experience with a reputation for being a very strong leader, and a healthy business performance for 2007 added further to his credentials.

A dilemma of a different kind confronted him the following year in the aftermath of the Sichuan earthquake. As described in Chapter 2, emotions were running high throughout the country, and the eyes of the people were on companies, particularly foreign companies. Much was expected of them, but it was hard to divine how much. The firm did earthquake-related pro-bono work, and undertook to match staff donations to disaster relief agencies on a one-for-one basis. But the pressure from blogs and other media was unrelenting. It became clear to the boss that 400,000 yuan—200,000 yuan contributed by employees, plus a matching contribution by the company—was not enough, and that the boss himself had to take the lead and show compassion and empathy.

Once again he consulted with his advisers, and they tested various numbers. Mindful of their advice, the boss decided he would match the total contributions of the staff (200,000 yuan) out of his own pocket, and the company would match his contribution in the same way as it had matched those of the staff. The total donations of the firm thus amounted to 800,000 yuan (200,000 from employees, matched by the company, plus 200,000 from the leader, also matched by the company). This was considered an appropriate sum for a firm of that size.

Problems of a different kind emerged the following year in 2009 as a consequence of the world financial crisis. Demand for the firm's services fell sharply at the end of 2008, and losses were incurred in January and February. Something had to be done, but the leader, in his "emperor," rather than CEO persona, was reluctant to deploy the standard western "right-sizing" solution of cutting headcount. He looked around him and saw 30 percent across-the-board salary cuts at SOEs, and reductions in CEO salaries at some private Chinese companies to a token 10 cents a month.

After consultations with advisers, he signed a contract with staff in which he promised not to fire anyone, and introduced an across-the-board salary reduction plan, with higher percentage reductions for the higher paid. When announcing the arrangement his theme was "Being brave and confident." The confidence was reflected in his promise to refund the salary cuts when the company returned to an adequate level of profitability, as it did later that year.

This illustrates how the Chinese management style, or at least some elements of it, is likely to leak out of China and exert influence on management styles elsewhere in the world. Remember, this is the Chinese WOFE of an EU-based parent company with offices all over the world. If employees in the US or UK subsidiaries, for example, like the idea of salary rather than headcount cuts in the event of a market downturn, they might be emboldened by the precedent set by the Chinese subsidiary to demand similar treatment.

Listen and learn

Constant environmental scanning is an integral part of the Chinese management model. Like the emperor leader in the story above, who looked around to see how other Chinese companies were handling the downturn, foreign managers must learn the art of looking for signs and listening for weak signals heralding major changes or pointing in new directions.

Government is the most important component of the Chinese business environment, so government-watching is the most important part of environmental scanning. Foreign firms must emulate their domestic rivals, and base their strategies, or rather "visions," and market positions on publicly stated priorities and intentions.

The Chinese Communist Party's (CCP's) "to do" list may change when the new government comes to power in 2012, but the longer-term priorities are not expected to differ substantially from those expressed in one way or another by the current administration. They include the following.

Industrial evolution

The government wants to encourage the development of an economy less dominated by agriculture and manufacturing, and foster the emergence of a strong service sector, including leisure and tourism. Clear evidence of the seriousness of this intent is provided by the Universal Studio and Disneyland projects in Beijing. Hotels are another area ripe for development. There are expensive high-end hotels in major cities, but as yet, no national budget hotel chains such as Accor for blue-collar workers, businesspeople, and budget tourists. This rebalancing will not be without its own problems. Local officials in a township near Beijing were heavily criticized in the press after seizing land from peasants, to build an artificial lake to attract tourists.

The government also sees as essential further modernization of the agricultural sector, including land reform, and larger and more professionally managed farms.

Welfare

Various policy priorities and intentions are embraced by President Hu Jintao's stated wish to create a "harmonious society." Improved health-care is one example. The government has been investing quite heavily in new hospitals for some time, but it also wants to widen coverage of the healthcare system, and of the welfare system as a whole. Wider health and welfare coverage is seen as a way to boost domestic demand. The high Chinese savings rate of 20–25 percent of disposable income is seen as a major reason why domestic demand is rising so slowly.

It is hoped that extended welfare coverage, including unemployment benefits, will reduce the savings ratio and thus increase domestic consumption, which should cause more of the wealth created during China's economic transformation to trickle down to rural areas and so contribute to a more harmonious society.

Healthcare reform should create opportunities for foreign firms in the healthcare sector. The government's wish to improve provisions for retirement offers opportunities in pensions, and moves to take some of the heat out of China's urban property boom by stimulating housebuilding should benefit a range of industries associated with housing.

Environmental protection and infrastructure

Environmental protection and clean infrastructure developments are also among current People's Republic of China (PRC) government priorities. This means heavy investments in clean and renewable energy systems, and a major expansion of public transport, including high-speed trains connecting the major cities. The latter is seen as a necessary part of the rebalancing of the economy, and is good news for western companies, because transport costs are a major problem in China.

Laws and regulation

The PRC will also be developing its regulatory and law enforcement systems in the coming years, to create a clearer statutory and regulatory environment for business, and to address problems related to business practices, corruption, and property rights. On economic management it will be reform its tax system further and refine its monetary policy controls.

Education

A theory of economic development proposed by Simon Kuznets in 1955 predicts that economic inequality will rise as a country develops, and then, after a critical average income is reached, will begin to fall.[3] The Kuznets curve, with time, economic development, or per-capita income on the horizontal axis, and some inequality measure such as the Gini coefficient on the vertical axis, is an inverted "U."

In the initial stages of economic development workers migrate from agriculture to industry and from rural areas to the towns. Because industry pays better than agriculture, inequality rises, but it falls thereafter if growth continues, because industry's hunger for ever more educated workers requires mass education, which is normally accompanied by other income redistribution processes.

The validity of the Kuznets curve has been called into question in recent years by rapidly rising inequality in developed economies, particularly the United States but the emphasis Kuznets placed on education is in tune with the Chinese government's own thinking. The lack of a properly educated and trained workforce is seen as a constraint on China's further economic development.

An article published on the PRC's Ministry of Education website in April 2010 suggests four long-term intentions:

- First, to raise the not yet attained 1993 target of investing 4 percent of GDP a year in education, to a proportion closer to the internationally recommended 6 percent of GDP. Within this huge prospective increase in total investment there would be a shift of educational investment from urban to rural areas. According to a recent UN Education for All Global Monitoring Report, spending per junior and middle school student is 18 times higher in Beijing and Shanghai than in the poorest provinces.
- Second, to develop an education system to match China's status as the third-largest world economy (in August 2010 China overtook Japan to become the world's second-largest economy) and "to meet the rising aspirations and expectations of the people," the PRC seems to recognize there is a good case for extending compulsory education from 9 to 12 years in line with industrialized nations.
- Third, to reduce China's 71 million illiterates in the 15-plus age group, of whom more than two-thirds are women, and particularly to reduce high illiteracy levels among ethnic minorities and rural populations.
- Fourth, to improve girls' and women's participation, retention, and achievement in education at all levels.

The quality of China's higher education is also a concern. There is a perception that universities are turning out graduates who are diligent and work long hours, but are not sufficiently creative to improve China's research and development capabilities and create a more innovative industrial sector. Since research indicates that the quantity and quality of innovation increase as GDP per capita rises, achieving a more "harmonious society" will help here. Business education and training is also seen as an area requiring improvement and expansion, and in an effort to stimulate innovation, subsidies are being provided for research and development.

In short, education is likely to be a strong growth area, offering plenty of opportunities for foreign businesses during the next two decades or so.

As a general rule, when trying to anticipate shifts in policy that might offer opportunities, foreign companies should identify the structural differences between China's economy now and the economy of supposedly developed economies, see them as areas likely eventually to attract remedial policy attention, and listen attentively for indications that policy apples of this kind to which they are well-equipped to contribute may be about to fall to the ground.

When UBS China chief Li Yi was talking with a few foreign business leaders, one of them said he needed to go to school. "We thought he was joking. He said he should study in Party School (Central Party School, see Chapter 5) for a year." Li was struck by the idea. "I asked him why. He said the country's policy-makers were there, and he needed to understand their minds, logic, and which cultural and political concepts they based their policies on. I think he has almost understood … when you enter a market have you understood its political, cultural, and historical environment?"

Engagement

Although China does not need their money any more, foreign investors are still welcome. They offer different perspectives, can provide access to new technology, and can introduce new business models, ideas, and approaches that may, or may not prove useful (see below). And they act as conduits for China's cultural and economic interaction with the outside world.

There is still "brand equity" in foreignness in other words, which an "old hand" of 20 years standing in China relinquishes at his or her peril. "Going native" is not an option, because you could lose your objectivity and alertness, and in any case, "going native" is not easy. In big cities such as Shanghai and Beijing, east and west seem close, and the gap between them seems bridgeable. Appearances are deceptive, however. The real Chinese culture lives a thousand feet below the urban surface, with its patina of western culture, and is inaccessible to foreign firms, however well-established they are in China.

But you need some sort of docking mechanism or adaptor plate; some way to engage with the Chinese culture and management style, which allows you to retain your own culture and style, while respecting and working effectively with those of your hosts. The differences between your cultures should be seen, not as problems to overcome, but as opportunities to gain new perspectives and create new value that could not otherwise have been created.

Docking, or engaging with the Chinese culture and management style, is necessary both between foreign and Chinese companies and within foreign companies operating in China.

External engagement

Part of the docking mechanism is access to networks. Foreign firms need to cultivate contacts among both administrators and merchants, and should always remember that, although they may be operating in provinces far from the capital, there is always a top man or woman based in Beijing.

In an article in the *Harvard Business Review* (*HBR*), a Harvard Business School professor, Lynn Paine, urged foreign companies operating in China to "understand the market, but work with the state."[4] She said that "in most industries, it's impossible to do well in China without the government's backing," and that in addition to making high-level connections, foreign companies must be able "demonstrate their projects' contribution to China's development."

Another aspect of the Chinese culture that must be accommodated is the pervasive influence of spirituality. Luxury goods are a case in point. The only people who buy them will be the newly rich. The older rich already have them, and will be deterred from buying more by spiritual themes in the culture, particularly in Confucianism, that frown on bragging and conspicuous consumption. The import and consumption of luxury goods will continue, but will grow much more slowly than in the past.

Foreign companies must also take into account growing concerns for the environment. A new tax on cars with engines of more than 3 liters is reshaping the market. It is no longer fashionable to own big cars, and there has been talk of a congestion charge in Beijing.[5]

Internal engagement

When problems arise in western companies, managed in a western way, the normal reaction of the company leader is to reach for packaged off-the-shelf, or more or less customized, solutions in the form of tools, methods, or processes often developed at business schools. This is how the art and science of western management develops. It is an axiom of western management that the application of tailored solutions to specific problems, and the embedding of the solutions in the wider management system, leads to a progressive improvement in the quality of management.

It seems to work, in the west at any rate. Mistakes are made. Some tools and processes are discarded when found to be ineffective, or counter-productive, but by and large the quality of management has steadily improved.

In her *HBR* article (see above) Lynn Paine advises the foreign CEOs of Chinese businesses to deal with health, safety, environmental, business ethics, and general business conduct issues by appointing "business practices officers" and "corporate integrity committees" to oversee investigations of misconduct, and setting up compliance processes and additional layers of monitoring. These are good first steps, because they convey the right messages and priorities, but there are two problems with this approach in a Chinese company.

The first is that such solutions, although they seem to be neutral and objective, and thus generally applicable, have been developed within a particular culture, which can be broadly characterized as English-speaking and Anglo-Saxon. This culture imposes its own set of moral, ethical, philosophical, and socio-economic constraints to which the tools and processes that emerge from it must necessarily be adapted. In other words, tools that work OK in the West might not work in China, or could have unexpected consequences in China when they come up against Chinese cultural constraints.

Chinese managers have an insatiable appetite for western tools and techniques, and there is no doubt that some of them work; but only when they have been adapted to the Chinese culture.

The second problem with western management tools and techniques in China is that the Chinese do not really like tools and processes in a business, which is, for them, equivalent to a family. They are OK with procedures, because they are like the duties and rituals (*li*) of Confucianism, but tools and processes are "unfamiliar"—better suited to the management of machines or mechanisms than members of a family.

Paine says that, to maintain high standards of business conduct in "the difficult Chinese environment," leaders must embed values in their organizations "not just through words and processes but also through deeds." This is fine as far as it goes, but it does not go far enough. As discussed in Chapter 3, in addition to "knowing" and "doing," business leaders in China must also cultivate the art of "being." The position of the "boss" in China is quite different from the position of CEOs in the West. It is not enough, in China, for bosses to know the corporate values and act in accordance with them. They must also embody them. If that is achieved, Confucian *li* (ritual), *xiao* (filial piety), and *zhong* (loyalty) will do more to maintain high standards of conduct than any number of processes or committees. Processes can be useful patches to provide time for an alignment of the *li*, but after that they are superfluous.

This is an aspect of another challenge for foreign leaders, related to the Chinese idea of a business as a family. They must play the roles expected of them. The CEO is the emperor, the patriarch, the creator of the vision, and the personification and guardian of the values, to whom employees owe a filial duty, and from whom they can expect paternal care and a share of the value they help to create. In the West, the employee has formal and "psychological" contracts with the company. In China, these contracts are with the leader.

An attribute of a Chinese leader is his or her *dong ban* (short for *dong shi zhang*, meaning chairman, and *ban gong shi*, meaning office), a personal support team, who filter information flows and protect the leader from unwelcome intrusions (see Chapter 9). The personal support team of Yuan Yafei, founder and chairman of HTSB (see page 101) exemplifies the Chinese *dong ban*. One example of a potentially useful fusion of the western and Chinese models is what might be called a "light" *dong ban*, which supports the leader Chinese-style while the leader's door remains "open" in the western style.

One engagement stratagem that has obvious attractions is to employ "sea-turtles"—ethnic Chinese people who have studied abroad, and can therefore straddle the cultural divide. Sea-turtles played a key role in bridging cultural gaps after Deng's opening-up in the 1980s, when the traffic was mainly from East to West, bringing the gospel of American management to China. They are less well equipped to bridge cultures now, when the important traffic is in the other direction. As Li put it:

> When they pursue further studies abroad they ... leave one school to join another without working experience in China ... [and] their studies abroad are highly segmented ... many sea turtles have only worked in one industry, or one part of the value chain, without a complete understanding of the industry.

He acknowledges their role in filling cultural and language gaps, but says the talent market is more open now, and many excellent people who have never studied abroad are emerging from China's population of 1.3 billion people.

Go with the flow

Creating value in China is becoming more difficult for all foreign companies. They are having to work harder in an environment that is becoming less and less like the American and European environments for business, and where the domestic competition is better adapted and growing stronger, smarter, and more self-assured by the day.

Foreign managers need to learn from their erstwhile students about the new way of doing business that is emerging in China, as if from the earth. Its familiarity is deceptive—a consequence of China's long, 30-year, now concluded American experiment. It borrows ideas and principles from the West when they seem useful, and they do not oppose or violate the spirit, land, energy trinity, but it adds up to a genuinely new way of doing business. Foreign companies do not have to go native and try to be Chinese, but they must understand the new style, insofar as it is understandable, and engage with it.

They must also recognize that they are going to have to raise their game to compete effectively with Chinese companies. They have been competing with kids for 30 years, but those kids have grown up now and are not competing purely on price. Quality and technology are no longer the exclusive preserves of foreign firms. Competition in China is becoming more like competition within Europe or America, with the added complication of a new management model and style to which foreign firms will find it hard to adapt.

Add to that misunderstandings arising from subtle cultural nuances below the threshold of occidental awareness, the abnormally high event-density caused by China's breathtaking economic growth, and the complexities created by spirit, land, energy interactions, and western managers working in China could be forgiven for feeling a little stressed from time to time. Take a cold shower. Clear your mind. Look on the bright side.

As that wise man travelling between the two towns implied, foreign firms that take a positive view of China and "go with the flow," as the Daoists advocate, should prosper.

Summary

- Whether or not foreign companies prosper in China will depend on their "set" to the country.
- They should first try to understand how their perceptions of China are influenced by their own management styles.
- China's management weaknesses are no longer a perfect match for the strengths of the western management style.
- Foreign business people operating in China should listen carefully to the voice of the "land" (the government).
- They need to engage effectively both externally and internally.
- They should become Daoists and "go with the flow."

Notes

1 "Business sours on China," *Wall Street Journal*, March 17, 2010.
2 Roland Berger (2009) *The European Management Approach. The Specifics and Advantages of Doing Business the European way*, March.
3 Kuznets, S. (1955) "Economic growth and income inequality," *American Economic Review*.
4 Paine, L. S. (2010) "The China rules," *Harvard Business Review*, June.
5 *China Daily*, October 30, 2009.

CHAPTER 9

Two roads ahead

There is nothing controversial, still less original, about the idea that China's transition from a developing to a developed economy is the defining geo-economic phenomenon of the twenty-first century. It was obvious to Napoleon Bonaparte two centuries ago that "When China wakes it will shake the world." The wonder is that it has taken so long.

It was much less obvious that in the process China's entrepreneurs would develop a way of doing business that differs significantly from what has, until now, been regarded as the standard management style or model. That such a development should have occurred in a country that for 30 years had modeled its way of doing business on the western style of management is all the more surprising.

There are standard ways to do things. There is not much scope, for example, for variation in the way you drive a car or ride a horse. For a long time it was assumed that the same was true of business; that the logic of the business situation prescribed one particular form of enterprise, and one particular style of management. And it was taken as self-evident that this form, and this style were most highly developed in the United States. Variations on the supposedly standard American style have appeared in Europe and Japan, but they are relatively minor and the process of globalization has progressively reduced their significance.

It has been argued in this book that the China variation is more significant; that its gradual emergence during the past few years marks an important departure from what had previously seemed to be the main sequence in the evolution of corporate management. It has also been suggested that, although the impact the China variation will have on business management elsewhere remains to be seen, it would still be a development of historic importance for businesses all over the world even if it were confined entirely to China.

This is not the conventional wisdom about where Chinese business is heading. Before ending with a restatement of the argument, let us look briefly at this conventional view.

The counter-argument

Some observers argue that although a new way of doing business may have emerged in China in recent years, it will not last. They say it is a transitional style of management that temporarily extends the limits of entrepreneurial leadership, but which will quickly reach its own limits. It will not scale up, in other words. If China's best private sector firms want to keep growing and establish themselves on the world stage, their management styles will have to return to the main sequence; to the standard western model.

The leadership style at most Chinese companies is autocratic, like the American leadership style, so this argument goes, but unlike their US counterparts, Chinese private-sector company leaders lack sufficient management strength in depth. To scale up further, they will need stronger, more professional managers and a more coherent management structure through which to implement strategy. This is the essential step from entrepreneurial to managerial leadership, which when taken will return the evolution of Chinese management to the main sequence.

Some of China's first-generation entrepreneurs are keenly aware of the significance of, and challenges posed by, this transition from an entrepreneurial to a managerial way of going business. It is a challenge of great concern, for example, to Zhang Lan, the founder of the South Beauty restaurant chain (see page 180).

An implication of this belief that the western management model is the natural model, the model required by the natural economic laws and logic that govern business and enterprise, is that management is a purely rational activity that transcends cultural differences and provides no place for the spiritual. The emphasis many Chinese entrepreneurs place on their cultural roots is thus a superficial and temporary adaptation, which will have to be dispensed with if the company is to emerge from the entrepreneurial stage. According to

Box 9.1 Zhang Lan

Chairman of South Beauty Co., Ltd

Zhang Lan
Source: South Beauty

A few years ago, Zhang Lan, founder of South Beauty, walked out of a television show on family businesses. She was very apologetic, but said "The topic doesn't fit me." South Beauty was a family business, in that Zhang's son was involved in it, but she had realized the show was about what Americans call "mom and pop," or "life-style" businesses, and Zhang saw South Beauty as a family business of quite a different kind. She left the show because she did not want to mislead people.

Founded in 2000, South Beauty Group (SBG) today consists of two up-market brands: South Beauty Restaurants, catering for the business elite, and STEAM, aimed at middle- to high-end urban consumers. It is the leading high-end restaurant company in China, and partly because it is managed as a portfolio of brands, rather than as a collection of separate businesses, it is thought to have the most development potential.

SBG is a cultural as well as a business success, because it serves Sichuan food, previously considered cheaper, more down-market than the Hong Kong-style cuisine. With well-designed restaurants, high-quality photographs in menus and excellent service, South Beauty successfully rebranded the Sichuan cuisine.

One of Zhang's greatest challenges when developing the company was attracting qualified professional managers. "It is more difficult for the catering industry to attract well-qualified managers than it is for emerging industries such as renewable energy and IT," she says. "We worked hard on this issue for many years, and managed to change the traditional view of catering." SBG's chief financial officer was hired from Google and its chief executive officer came from a western consultancy firm.

Another perception Zhang has helped to change is that family firms are run by families. "In China, people have the impression that in family firms, family members always work in the key positions. But that has proved to be inefficient in Europe." Zhang studied cross-cultural management in London, and traveled in Europe examining family businesses. She found that successful family firms employed professional managers. Family members are shareholders and are not usually directly involved in management, so there is space for the development of professional management cultures. If problems arise that prove beyond the professional manager's ability to resolve, a family member may step in to sort them out, as in the case of Akio Toyoda, grandson of the founder of the Toyota Company, in 2008.

Following her research into European family firms, Zhang committed herself to cultivating the conditions in South Beauty required for the development of professional managers. This included, among other things, substantial investment in training and installing an enterprise resource planning system.

Zhang's interest in long-lived family firms is personal as well as professional. Like many first-generation Chinese entrepreneurs she has children in their 20s, to whom she would like to hand over the management reins at South Beauty at some stage. Her research into European family firms has convinced her that well-managed family-owned firms can prosper for generations. She wants South Beauty to go on for 100 years.

In Zhang's view, the positions of western and Chinese professional managers differ in several important respects. The environment for professional managers in Europe is easier and more secure than in China, and some professional managers prefer to work for unlisted family companies, because of the absence of constant pressure from capital markets for continuous improvements in performance. Things are less stable and secure in China for professional managers, and jobs are less easy to find. There are more opportunities, however, to help to build a company and develop a brand in a short space of time.

She thinks the environment for business in China is favorable for rapid development. "It took some European retail groups 100 years to establish themselves as famous brands," she says. "It has taken South Beauty just 10 years." But she does not intend to expand too fast, because her studies of western family firms have shown that long-lived brands take time to become firmly established. She says some Chinese businesspeople are in too much of a hurry.

SBG's brand-driven approach, using the themes of "quality, innovation, tradition," has proved very effective, both in attracting professional managers with compatible personal brands likely to enhance the corporate brand, and in giving SBG a competitive advantage. Zhang acknowledges that, in South Beauty's early years, her own personality and reputation were important marketing assets for the company. She does some advertising, because it is helpful for brand awareness, but believes that the reputation of a company depends more on the nature and quality of its operations. Most of the marketing effort these days is in product design and customer relationship management. Zhang thinks her personal brand and SBG's corporate brand continue to support each other, however.

Zhang went to study in Canada in 1989 and worked part time in a restaurant. This experience, and subsequent travels in Europe, have left her with the impression that China is misunderstood by foreigners. "Some westerners think pigs can fly in China; others think that the Cultural Revolution erased all our history, culture, and heritage." There is no "flying pig" on any of South Beauty's menus, but there is plenty of Chinese culture in the business as well as the cuisine.

Luyang Jiang and the author

this view, Jack Ma's *Tai Chi quan* demonstrations at conferences and employee meetings, and Feng Jun's "six wins" principle, are just marketing; employee, and public relations veils behind which the real business of business proceeds unaffected, in its rational and culturally neutral way.

It is recognized that the standard management style must be adapted to some extent to local environments, and pay lip service to local and national cultures. But these adaptations do not run deep enough to change the basic model in any fundamental way. As the company grows, acquires a life of its own independent of its founders, and becomes dependent on international capital markets, and integrated with the global economy, it will have to put away these attributes of youth and immaturity.

Another way of making the same point is to argue that the emerging Chinese management model has been protected from the consequences of its intrinsic inefficiencies by its separation hitherto from the global marketplace. It will not survive for long, according to this view, when it begins to compete internationally with the more efficient western model. This is the evolutionists' "speciation by separation" idea, also known as the Galapagos syndrome. China's management model and style, like the models of birds and reptiles in the Galapagos Islands, have, until now, been free to find their own evolutionary paths, untouched by evolution elsewhere. Although there are some obvious flaws in this argument—Chinese firms have been deeply touched by western management models ever since Deng's opening-up in 1978—it may have merit when applied to China's state-owned enterprises (SOEs).

Thus the argument in this book and the counter-argument summarized above see two quite different roads ahead for Chinese management: continuing divergence from the supposed "main sequence" on the one hand, leading to a distinctively Chinese model, and a shift in the current direction of development towards convergence with the main sequence on the other hand, as Chinese private-sector firms emerge from the entrepreneurial stage, leading to reunification with the American model that guided China's entrepreneurs for 30 years.

In practice, some Chinese companies will choose one road and some will choose the other. They will begin to compete with one another for markets, resources, and people. The debate between the argument in this book and the counter-argument will be settled by which of the two competing approaches prevails in China over the next three decades or so.

Styles as expressions of cultures

One of the main weaknesses of the counter-argument is that it sees China through western eyes, and implicitly assumes that the model of management that will become standard in China is emerging from an environment that is the same as, or similar to, the environment that shaped the western style of management.

Some will deny this is an implicit assumption, and will insist that the original environments are irrelevant; that the western style evolved because it is better than all other styles, and has since demonstrated its superiority in the marketplace. But there is no evidence for this assertion. As we saw in Chapter 3, the American style and the organizational form within which it evolved were the creatures of accident and environment, rather than the inexorable working-out of natural economic law. If, for example, the electric telegraph had been introduced to the American railroads just a few years earlier, things might have turned out differently.

The environment of modern China is very different from that of the United States in the late nineteenth century. To suppose that, in the absence of any foreign model, the style of management that evolved in China would have been the same as the style that evolved in America, is to be guilty of unwarranted ethnocentrism. It is likely that the mature Chinese multinational will resemble the mature US multinational on the outside, as the whale, in adapting to its marine environment, came to resemble the fish on the outside, in an example of what is known as "convergent evolution." But the whale remained a mammal.

When pondering the impact of culture on the evolution of models or styles of management, unanswerable "what if?" questions arise. What management models or styles would have evolved, for instance, had the Babylonian, Egyptian, or Roman civilizations survived? In what ways would they differ, if at all, from the models and styles used today? Those who subscribe to the idea that natural selection over the millennia would have caused management styles that emerged in different civilizations to converge on one standard style will say there would be no differences. Others would predict differences of more or less significance, depending on how responsive and open to outside influences the surviving civilization had been.

This book subscribes to the second view. It argues that culture is a sculptor of ways of doing business, as well as ways of life, and that China's culture, which was for long periods relatively closed to outside influence, is producing a management style that differs significantly from the western style.

When comparing the cultural origins of American and Chinese styles of management, the most striking difference is age—two centuries versus three millennia. Some say that the Cultural Revolution (1966–71) erased much of China's culture from folk memory, and thus left a more or less empty canvas for the American experiment. There may be some truth in this, but that was then. China's folk memory has since been culturally refreshed, and perhaps partly because of its suppression, it has acquired a value and significance for ordinary Chinese people not enjoyed by other cultures.

The management style now emerging from China's culture is a hybrid in the sense that it incorporates ideas and principles from western management styles and traditions. But it is not a pastiche.

What it borrows from elsewhere must "fit." The hybrid is thus an authentic expression of the Chinese culture. How competitive it will prove in the struggle of style against style in the global economy will depend, among other things, on whether three distinctive qualities of the Chinese style turn out to be advantages or disadvantages.

Spirit, land, energy

How things turn out will depend partly on how conflicts that arise when the supposedly "standard" western management model confronts China's spirit, land, energy trinity are resolved. Both will adapt to the other, of course, but which one will prevail when the scope for compromise is finally exhausted? The argument in this book has been that the Chinese "trinity" will prevail. The counter-argument implies the opposite.

Those who support the counter-argument misjudge the permanence and power of the spirit, land, energy trinity. It is the rock on which alien cultures that cannot accommodate or adapt to it are bound to founder.

"China is like a company, 51 percent owned by the government," said a Chinese businessman. "The chairman [president] and CEO [premier] have control. Everyone else is a minority shareholder. Obama [the US president] owns no shares. In China the boss is also the major shareholder. The government and entrepreneurs also share the same values. It's the emperor model; the majority shareholder model. In China people need to work for a better life for the boss, who then gives back."

Those who subscribe to the counter-argument are also mistaken when they see the use Chinese entrepreneurs make of culture and spirit as mere marketing. In most cases, there is nothing disingenuous or devious about it. References to culture (the *I Ching*, Daoism, *Tai chi*, Confucianism, and so on) resonate powerfully with employees, but that is not why Chinese entrepreneur leaders make such references. They mean it. It is not "spin." It reflects a belief that business in general and their companies in particular have emerged from, and are to an important extent expressions of, China's culture. They are latter-day "merchants" continuing their age-old dance with "administrators," and when they think about the legacies they will leave behind, being true to the culture and reinterpreting it for the modern age might matter more to many of the current generation of Chinese entrepreneurs than the accumulation of wealth.

Maximizing shareholder value may be a more rational and in a sense a "truer" definition of the purpose of a company, but if employees are not moved by it they will not follow. And administrators could not care less about a company's shareholders when deciding whether or not a project they are being asked to support or sponsor is in the interests of China. In other words, there are striking differences in the stakeholder "pecking order" in Chinese and western firms. A western CEO owes their first allegiance to shareholders, then to customers, then suppliers, and then employees. In China, country and community (employees and society at large) come first, even in the case of listed companies. Shareholders are seldom mentioned.

The boss

The role of the boss is another area where the counter-argument is based on a misunderstanding. The counter-argument sees the Chinese CEO as an autocrat, and predicts that the Chinese management style will return to the main sequence as Chinese companies grow and the scale limits of autocratic management are reached. But although they are "bosses," Chinese CEOs are not autocrats, in the sense implied by the counter-argument. Chinese CEOs can and do delegate to less conspicuous, but no less able executives, and as explained in Chapter 7, a distinguishing feature of the Chinese management style is a consensus-seeking quality that requires proposals for a change in direction to be discussed thoroughly beforehand.

The position of "boss" is essential in the well-ordered Confucian society or institution, but in becoming boss the boss acknowledges obligations to the bossed under the Mandate of Heaven (see Chapter 7). The boss is more like a chairperson with a casting vote than an autocrat or an all-powerful US-style CEO. The boss position has to be occupied, but there is no requirement for bosses to act like tyrants motivated entirely by their own interests.

In her 'China rules' article in the *Harvard Business Review* (see page 172), Lynn Paine quotes a Yuan dynasty proverb: "An army of a thousand is easy to find, but, ah, how difficult to find a general."[1] It is true the shoes of a Chinese key leader are harder to fill than those of an American CEO. The model requires special skills that are hard to teach, and cannot be acquired by everyone. But in such a large country, with such a long tradition of imperial rule, men and women of this kind are sure to emerge from to time, just as they do in America.

Steve Jobs, boss of Apple, is very "Chinese" in many ways. He is a showman like Jack Ma of Alibaba (see page 124) who, like Zhang Lan of South Beauty (see page 180), uses his personal brand to support the corporate brand. He is much admired within and outside Apple, inspires enviable employee and customer loyalty, and although he is said to be far from easy to work with, he has assembled around him a multi-talented team who support and acknowledge the value of the company's key leader.

Understood in this way, the key leader in any Chinese organization is not the constraint on further growth, or on the transition from an entrepreneurial to a managerial stage of development, that the counter-argument supposes it to be.

Moreover, the CEO of a large Chinese company will usually assemble a well-staffed private office (*dong ban*), which acts much like the office of palace clerks assembled by the sixth Han emperor, Wu Di, in the second century BC (see Chapter 4). The *dong ban* should not be confused with the executive committee of the western model. It usually comprises a varied group of able people entirely dedicated to the service of the CEO/emperor. Its role is to extend the CEO's reach, and project his or her power. It stands between the CEO and the outside world, protecting him or her from flows of unfiltered information and unwanted intrusion. Its members act as gatekeepers and emissaries. In a conversation between two companies the initial exchanges are between *dong ban* and *dong ban*.

Scale

Another questionable assumption in the counter-argument is that it is the destiny of all Chinese small and medium-sized enterprises (SMEs), and the desire of all their leaders, to become *Fortune 500*-scale multinationals, and it is thus necessary for them to dispense with any qualities or aspects of their management style that might inhibit their ability to grow.

No doubt many Chinese CEO/entrepreneurs do dream of joining the 33 mainland Chinese state-owned enterprises in the 2009 *International Fortune 500* list. But few of them will have detailed strategies featuring a series of major acquisitions to realize such dreams. They are not great long-term planners. They have dreams, but although they talk about "strategy," because westerners expect them to, they do not do it. What may seem like a great strategy in retrospect is often the outcome of a more or less random walk, through a landscape full of opportunities, where each step creates new possibilities.

Strategy-light companies of this kind do not need as large staff functions or as elaborate managerial hierarchies as strategy-led western companies, and can therefore grow larger with less senior management. The main requirement in strategy-light firms is not an ability to formulate and implement strategic plans, but an ability to spot opportunities and react to them quickly.

Another assumption about scale implicit in the counter-argument is that for a modern economy to be judged "mature," it needs a decent complement of very large, integrated companies and that in making this judgment, SOEs do not count. In other words a complement of large integrated private companies is necessary evidence of maturity. As suggested in Chapter 7, given the inter-firm coordination made possible by modern web-based communication technology, this assumption is also questionable. It may be that, in a genuinely "modern" industrial economy unburdened by corporate legacies from the pre-digital age, an optimum distribution of firm size would be skewed more to the left than is the current western distribution, and that SMEs would account for a considerably larger proportion of total output.

China's growing pains

There is some evidence to suggest that China's business culture is relatively weak in some crucial areas such as creativity, the rate of innovation, brand-building, and financial performance. Corruption and low quality standards in some industries, such as toys, have also been identified by the Chinese government as areas in need of reform and improvement (see Chapter 2).

There are also structural problems in the labor market associated with the demographic consequences of China's one-child policy, and a lack of affordable urban housing.

These problems were highlighted in summer 2010 by two stories made much of in the western press: an apparent suicide "cluster" at the 300,000-employee Shenzhen factory of Foxconn Technology Group, the world's largest electronics contract manufacturer, and strikes for higher wages at Honda's plants in southern China.

The suicide cluster story turned out to be something of a storm in a teacup. Apple's CEO, Steve Jobs, and others pointed out that the suicide rate at the Shenzhen factory of the Taiwan-based Foxconn, which employs 800,000 people and counts Apple, Sony, Dell, Nokia, and Hewlett-Packard among its main clients, is actually lower than China's national average. The publicity had an effect, however. Soon after the suicide story broke, Foxconn's chairman Terry Gou announced a 30 percent increase in basic pay at Foxconn's Chinese plants to 1,200 yuan a month, and barely a week later he promised another rise in October to 2,000 yuan (US$293) a month at the Shenzhen plant.

These pay rises and the strikes for higher wages at Honda's plants (most of the labor unrest in summer 2010 was at foreign-owned companies) are seen as ominous signs of a tightening of the labor market and the beginnings of an erosion of China's international labor costs advantage. Looked at in another way, there is nothing ominous about them. On the contrary, they are precisely what one would expect in a maturing industrial economy, and are best seen as early signs of a long-term shift in the distribution of value added from capital to labor, and thus an important, symbolic step towards realizing President Hu's dream of an "harmonious society."

Foreign firms need to watch these developments carefully. China is changing all the time. As some doors close, others are opening. As coastal labor markets tighten, manufacturers are moving inland in search of cheaper labor. Domestic demand is gradually taking over from exports as the primary growth engine. Perceived weaknesses in such areas as creativity, innovation, brand-building, quality, and financial management offer opportunities for foreign firms in the medium term, but will gradually be made good in the longer term as empty niches in China's economy are occupied by local players, and internal competition intensifies.

China's economy is a work in progress, but it is already clear that when it is "finished," or rather (because economies and societies are never finished) when it reaches a level of maturity comparable to that of western economies, it will be very different. People feel much closer to their values in China. The widespread interest in *Tai chi,* Daoism, and Confucianism cannot be dismissed or ignored as a fashion that will fade, or as mere marketing.

This is the central challenge for westerners. They must resist the temptation, despite the encouragement to do so being given to them by some Chinese, to see Chinese businesses as straying temporarily from the main sequence, and try to nudge them back on track. It is no longer possible, if it ever was, to mold China in the western image. China is changing, but it cannot be changed by outsiders. It is going its own way, finding its own solutions to its problems, and developing its own approaches and its own management style. It does not react well to attempts to impose other solutions and other styles. It needs to be understood and dealt with as it is, not as westerners would like it to be.

Westerners must learn from previous attempts to mold China in the western image and impose on the Chinese their own approaches and models of acceptable behavior and commercial conduct.

Failure to communicate

The Opium Wars (1839–42 and 1856–60) were the culmination of trade disputes between China under the Qing dynasty and the United Kingdom. This was not the last time that trade issues—in this case, a lack of Chinese demand for British goods, and an insatiable appetite in Britain for Chinese tea, silk, and porcelain—would affect China's relationships with other countries. British merchants were obliged to pay for the goods with silver, because it was the only currency the Chinese would accept. This was no basis for a stable long-term trading relationship. Britain's problem was aggravated by the fact that it had adopted the gold standard and so had to buy its silver from other European countries to finance its trade deficit.

Despite protests from the Qing government, British merchants began to export opium from India to China. It was an effective solution to the trade gap, and the flow of silver was reversed. Concerned by the growing number of addicts, China's emperor prohibited the sale and smoking of opium in 1729 for all but medicinal purposes.

In defeating the French at Plassey in 1757, the English East India Company (EEIC) acquired an effective monopoly in the production of Indian opium, and it identified China as an important market, despite the Qing's prohibition. So began an episode in British history for which the word "inglorious" might have been invented.

EEIC merchants devised an ingenious stratagem to evade China's ban on opium imports. They bought tea in Canton (Guangzhou) on credit, and balanced their books by selling opium at auction in Calcutta. The narcotic was hidden on British ships, carried to the Chinese coast, and smuggled ashore by Chinese dealers. EEIC opium exports to China are estimated to have grown from about 15 tons in 1730 to about 75 tons in 1773.

The Qing government reaffirmed the prohibition in 1799 and issued a decree in 1810 that began "Opium has a harm. Opium is a poison, undermining our good customs and morality. Its use is prohibited by law." But it was unable to stop the smuggling. By 1838 the British were selling an estimated 1,400 tons a year to China.

In March 1839, the Emperor appointed a commissioner, Lin Zexu, to control the opium trade at the port of Canton. Lin first insisted that the imperial prohibition be respected. When the EEIC traders ignored his demand, he arrested 1,600 foreign merchants and Chinese traffickers, and confiscated 11,000 pounds of opium. Charles Elliot, Britain's trade superintendent, tried to negotiate a compromise, but Lin seized 20,000 crates of opium from foreign-owned warehouses, held foreign merchants under arrest until they surrendered another large amount of the drug, which was then burned, and declared the port of Canton closed to foreign merchants.

This was one provocation too far. Elliot ordered a blockade of the Pearl River, and in the ensuing naval battle in November 1839, the Royal Navy sank several Chinese vessels near Canton. On receiving news of the outbreak of hostilities, the British government sent a large British Indian army, which landed in southern China in June 1840. By January 1841 the British had captured the Bogue forts at the mouth of the Pearl River and controlled the high ground above Canton. By June, following victories at Ningbo and Chinhai against the ill-equipped and poorly trained imperial army, they controlled most of southern China. The emperor sued for peace. and the Treaty of Nanjing was signed in August 1842. It obliged China to pay reparations, open four ports to Britain, and cede Hong Kong to Queen Victoria. In 1844, the United States and France concluded similar treaties with China.

Although Lin Zexu's strong attack on the opium trade failed and he was made a scapegoat by the emperor for provoking British military retaliation, he is now seen as a hero of nineteenth-century China, for his principled stand against European imperialism.

Friction between British merchants and Chinese officials grew over the ensuing decade. Hostilities resumed in 1856, after the Chinese searched a suspicious British ship. The British laid siege to the treaty port of Canton in late 1856, and after making common cause with the French, who were involved in a separate dispute with the Chinese, moved against the five Taku forts leading to Beijing. The Second Opium War ended with ratification of the Treaty of Tianjin in 1860. It involved the creation of 10 new open ports, permission for foreigners (including Protestant and Catholic missionaries) to travel throughout China, and indemnities to Britain and France.

These were wars out of time; incongruous outbreaks of mercantilist aggression in a capitalist age. They initiated China's "century of humiliation," which would culminate in the events of May 4, 1919 and the subsequent emergence of modern China. They disgusted English liberals. The First Opium War was attacked in the House of Commons by recently elected Member of Parliament William Ewart Gladstone, destined to become one of Britain's most illustrious prime ministers. He said, "a war more unjust in its origin, a war more calculated to cover this country with permanent disgrace, I do not know."

There was no meeting of minds here; no attempt by either party to understand the other's position. Opium for recreational use did not become illegal in Britain until 1868, but its harmful effects were known long before then. The right of China's ruler to protect his people from what he saw as dangerous addiction by making the drug illegal was surely undeniable. The ability of Britain to protect the interests of EEIC merchants by military force should have been equally obvious to the Qing emperor.

It is 150 years since the end of the Second Opium War: long enough for all westerners to have learned that attempts to impose western business models and practices on an increasingly unreceptive local business community will be counter-productive, and effort should be invested, instead, in understanding the Chinese and their business interests. Finally, it is not who wins the battle of business ideas that really matters. It is whether foreign firms can find ways to prosper in China, by contributing to China's economic development.

And who knows? It is not beyond the bounds of possibility that, in seeking ways to prosper in China, western firms may inadvertently stumble across management models or ideas that could improve their ability to prosper elsewhere.

Going abroad

Another export route for this emerging Chinese management style is through the international expansion of Chinese companies. This is an ambition shared by many first-generation Chinese entrepreneurs. Zhang Lan of South Beauty (see page 180) and Zhang Yong of Haidilao Hotpot (see page 69) both want to open restaurants in Europe.

There are difficulties, however, in addition to the usual problems of an inability to feel the pulses of local markets and detachment from China's history and culture. The first is to do with the role of the boss. The fact that Chinese companies are monolithic, in the sense that there is only one key leader, means that their overseas operations can be outposts, or branches, but never self-sufficient subsidiaries, and they will always be far from the centre and from the "emperor."

This is why it is said that "the journey to internationalization starts in China." The international divisions of many large Chinese firms are dominated by their domestic divisions, for which they usually act as little more than conduits for exports. Foreign acquisitions offer the possibility of replacing the incumbent local management team with Chinese managers well connected with the emperor and his *dong ban*. But this often ends badly, with low morale at the foreign company and the departure of key people.

Another option is to leave the incumbent managers in place and try to school them into the corporate culture, with visits to China and regular meetings with the emperor. This usually works better, and is probably the best that can be done, for the time being, because you cannot export a finished copy of an unfinished original.

Better management for a better world

The financial crisis of 2007–08 and its aftermath were major blows to the self-confidence of western managers, and to the confidence of western people in the western management system. The idea that western ways of doing business were the best of all possible ways was called into doubt. Something was seriously wrong, particularly in the banking sector. Company leaders came to be seen as reckless and overpaid, and the call went out for a return to the traditional virtues of prudence and frugality.

A common response, in the West, to popular demands for more frugal company leadership was the public announcement that top executives would henceforth travel economy rather than business class. It was not a common response in China. The idea that the "emperor" should suffer the indignities and discomforts of economy class and so compromise his or her ability to work en route and perform well on arrival would make no sense to Chinese people. It would be seen as an empty gesture that would save the company very little money, and do nothing to alleviate the pain of headcount reductions, or spread more evenly other privations made essential by the economic downturn.

A much more convincing demonstration of a leader's solidarity with the led, and concern for the "corporate family," would be to eschew headcount reductions as long as possible, and instead reduce staff costs by across-the-board salary reductions. This was the standard response to the economic downturn in China in both the private and state-owned sectors. It reflected a view of the relationships in a business enterprise between the top executives and other employees that differs significantly from the western view.

If as suggested in Chapter 8 such a response to economic downturns was to leak out of China, through foreign-owned Chinese companies, and establish itself as a new standard in western management, many would see this as a thoroughly healthy reversal of the traditional flow of influence between western and Chinese business cultures.

The "student" could become the teacher in other areas too, such as the emphasis Chinese managers place on vision and tactics, and the relatively low importance they attach to strategy; or the focus on group, rather than individual performance.

The Chinese still have much to learn about business and management from the West, of course, but it is no longer a one-way street, and in the end, good management, whatever its provenance, will tend to drive out bad management in an increasingly interconnected global economy.

At a time of doubt and questioning, in the West, about the role of business in society and the way in which companies are managed, it is sensible to look around the world for other models and options that might offer, if not a way out, at least new angles on some of the problems relating to business with which western societies are currently preoccupied.

The emerging Chinese style of management is a different model, and could offer pointers of this kind. It is still in its fetal stage, of course, but the fetus shows every sign of being viable, and its development in the years ahead will be worth studying. The aim of this book has been to draw attention to, and describe some aspects of, the new way of doing business emerging in China, in the hope that others may be inspired to examine it and its implications in more detail. It is not a way of doing business that will suit every company, in every country, but it looks as if it could become the standard way of doing business in one very important country, with which every foreign company with global ambitions will probably have to engage in one way or another.

Western businesses are not often minded to look further than their top and bottom lines, but the mutual understanding that can emerge from the day-to-day interactions between businesses from different cultures can do more in the long run to promote harmony within the society of nations than any amount of diplomacy. Whether business people are aware of it or not, it is to them, the ways they deal with and engage with each other, and the efforts they make to understand each other, that we must all look for prosperity within nations and peace between them.

Note

1 Paine, L. S. (2010) "The China rules," *Harvard Business Review*, June.